TREVOR'S PLACE

Trevor's Place

THE STORY OF THE BOY WHO BRINGS HOPE TO THE HOMELESS

Frank and Janet Ferrell
with Edward Wakin

1817

Harper & Row, Publishers, San Francisco

Cambridge, Hagerstown, New York, Philadelphia
London, Mexico City, São Paulo, Singapore, Sydney

For information regarding Trevor's Campaign address
P.O. Box 21
Gladwyne, Pennsylvania 19035.

TREVOR'S PLACE. *The Story of the Boy Who Brings Hope to the Homeless.* Copyright ©1985 by Frank and Janet Ferrell. Afterword copyright ©1985 by Rebecca J. Laird. All rights reserved. Printed in the United States of America. No part of this book may be used or reproduced in any manner whatsoever without written permission except in the case of brief quotations embodied in critical articles and reviews. For information address Harper & Row, Publishers, Inc., 10 East 53rd Street, New York, NY 10022. Published simultaneously in Canada by Fitzhenry & Whiteside, Limited, Toronto.

FIRST EDITION

Library of Congress Cataloging in Publication Data

Ferrell, Frank.
    Trevor's place.

    1. Ferrell, Trevor. 2. Youth volunteers in social service—Pennsylvania—Philadelphia—Biography. 3. Homelessness—Pennsylvania—Philadelphia—Case studies. I. Ferrell, Janet. II. Wakin, Edward. III. Title.

HV4506.P45F47 1985   362.5'8'0924 [B]   84–48768
ISBN 0-06-062531-7

85 86 87 88 89 RRD 10 9 8 7 6 5 4 3 2 1

Contents

With the exception of the Ferrell family and certain other major characters, names, places, and details have been changed.

Acknowledgments

We could never adequately acknowledge everyone who has made this book possible. Each volunteer, donor, editor, and friend leaves a visible mark on the book and on our lives. Using the words of Mother Teresa, each person's help has been but a drop in the bucket of inspiration and hard work, but even one drop would have been sorely missed.

The Sheraton Hotels have kindly provided accommodations when we have traveled. The Peace Mission gave us our home for the homeless, and the media promoted the positive news of helping others. We wish to credit them all for their efforts.

We feel a special indebtedness to the homeless themselves, who welcomed us into their world and accepted us fully before we were able to do the same for them.

Three more special people: Liza, Allen, and Jody, our beloved children, paid a painful price behind the scenes and came to not just tolerate but actively serve Trevor's Campaign. We thank God for their lives and support.

And, of course, we thank Trevor for listening to his heart and showing us the way, and we praise Jesus for keeping us strong.

Frank and Janet Ferrell
May 1985

1
The Beginning:
A Pillow and a Yellow Blanket

"Click." As I heard the lock drop on the door of the brown station wagon, I looked back and caught the apprehension in Janet's eyes. A chill went through me as I turned to watch the silhouette of Trevor, our eleven-year-old son, as he stepped silently toward the subway steam grate beside the white concrete building not five feet in front of where I stood on the curb.

The huddled body Trevor approached on the sidewalk was almost lost in the chilly darkness on the corner of 15th and Moravian Streets. A man in dirty pants and plaid shirt, his head cradled in his right arm, was lying there like a discarded newspaper. Although we were in the center of Philadelphia near the exclusive Union League Club, two-and-a-half weeks before Christmas, we might as well have been on a deserted Skid Row intersection. We were there alone with that shoeless man, staring at his grease-stained white socks, wondering whether he was unconscious or, worse, ready to explode with rage.

The man did not move from the steamy grate. The air that wafted up from underground surrounded him in a damp cloud of warmth.

I stood frozen. My own breath veiled my view as it turned to fog in the silent chill of a December evening. Each time I inhaled, the stench of sewage filled my head. An unseen rat scurried in between Trevor and me. I felt an eerie, nauseating churning in my stomach.

What had I allowed Trevor to talk us into? Why did I agree to come downtown tonight? As I read the graffiti that covers the alley walls behind the streets where business people and lawyers spend their daylight hours, I kept asking myself the same question. What are we doing here? What am I doing standing on a deserted corner clutching only a spare pillow, while my little son walks alone to that human form on the ground? I was clutching Trevor's special pillow, the one he needed to hug in order to fall asleep at night.

Trevor had pulled the hood of his jacket over his head and was a small dark figure in front of me. He walked hunched down as he approached the dozing form on the grate.

Only an hour before, Janet and I had been sipping coffee in the kitchen of our sixteen-room suburban ranch house. We chatted quietly as we looked out onto our kidney-shaped swimming pool and the darkness behind it that was our two acres of woodland. On that Thursday night it had felt particularly warm and cozy inside. Our children—Liza, Allen, Jody, and Trevor—were each in their own rooms. It was one of those nights when we were all at home, and we felt most like a family. All together, sheltered in our own cocooned, predictable world.

Suddenly, Trevor rushed in. "Quick, turn on the TV," he said breathlessly. He flipped through all the channels once, then twice. What he had seen was gone.

"The TV had these pictures of people who were living on the street!" Trevor exclaimed.

"Go on, Trevor," I prompted.

"So, do people really live like that? I thought they lived like that in India, but not here, I mean in America. The TV said these people live like that here in Philadelphia. They said it was especially sad because we're supposed to be the city of brotherly love!"

Trevor couldn't believe it. It couldn't be true.

"People sure do live like that, right in center city," I confirmed.

"Why are they there?" he persisted. His dark blue eyes clouded with confusion.

"Must be because they want to be," I said without thinking.

"You mean they have no place to sleep, no home?" He looked around the room in disbelief. "They're out there in the cold and snow right now? Tonight?"

"Trevor, not *everyone* lives the way we do here in Gladwyne." I turned back toward Janet to resume our conversation. But Trevor's interrogation continued.

"If they live on the streets, where do they eat? How do they stay alive without a bed or blanket when they sleep outside in the winter?" Janet and I answered as best we could—with vague, evasive answers. We didn't know.

"Well, can we go downtown and help them?" Trevor asked pointedly.

"Why not?" I expected that Trevor's impulse would soon go away, like most of them did.

"Why not tonight?" Trevor demanded.

"Oh, not tonight," I groaned. "I've had an awful day." The hassles at my electronics store in nearby Bala Cynwyd had been enough to deal with for one day.

Hoping to satisfy Trevor, Janet added, "Let's talk about it another time and we'll see about going downtown."

Trevor insisted. He wanted to go downtown tonight. He acted as if some street person's life depended on it.

Finally, I said, "That's *enough*, Trevor," and he dejectedly trudged back to his room. He was sad his own parents didn't want to help him help the people on the streets.

Janet and I looked at each other with a sigh. "Frank, we take all four of our kids to church and Sunday School every week and send them to Christian camp every summer because we want them to care about other people. What kind of double message are we giving him now?"

"I know, Janet," I responded. "I was just thinking about the discussion in our church group a few weeks ago. Remember? We talked about what it means to really love our neighbors and not just talk about it."

A rare opportunity to go with our son to give to the "least of these" was open before us. Trevor had initiated it. My eyes were drawn back to the cold darkness beyond our back patio. We lapsed into a long period of silence.

I thought maybe this would show Trevor, living in protected suburbia, how well off he was. Normally, he was all wrapped up in Pac-Man and riding his motorbike up and down the cul-de-sac. He was not working hard enough in school. We struggled with him all the time about his homework and grades. Maybe an experience like this would help him understand priorities and motivate him.

"OK, Trevor," I called out. I felt as though we were giving in to his childish impulse and just looking for adult justifications to rationalize going. "We'll take you downtown *to-night*." I was confident this would be the last we would hear of it.

As Trevor ran to find his warmest jacket and shoes, Janet dug an old yellow blanket out of the hall linen closet. Just as we were leaving, Trevor grabbed his special pillow from his bed. During the twelve-mile drive downtown, he put the blanket under the heater to warm it, and he quietly hugged the pillow.

Janet and I tried to prepare Trevor for what he would encounter downtown, not sure ourselves what we would discover. We weren't even sure that we would be able to find any street people. We didn't really know where to look.

We passed the expressway sign that directed us toward city center, and veered to the left.

"Now, Trevor," I said, "we may not even find anybody. And if we do, they may not want your blanket. If they don't want it, don't be upset. It has nothing to do with you. Some people have too much pride to accept charity."

I could tell Janet was worried about whether Trevor might

get injured. So I said, "Don't worry, Trevor, when we get down there, I'll be right behind you." But Trevor wasn't concerned at all.

Almost as soon as we arrived downtown, we saw the man sleeping on a grate at the corner of 15th and Moravian. We stopped the car and scrutinized the huddled figure. None of us had ever taken much notice of a street person, much less watched another human being sleep on the street. I marveled that he slept with nothing but metal strips beneath him . . . nothing to protect him from the bitter wind. I wondered what he dreamed of. I had never stared at another human being as I did that night. Who was he? Did he have any family? Friends? Where did he come from? How did he start out and how did he end up like this? Would he answer if we asked him questions? What will he do when Trevor steps up next to him? What kind of father am I to bring my son down here and then let him go over to some guy lying in the street? These thoughts raced through my head as we watched that mysterious human being, an isolated creature. At that moment the whole universe seemed to center on that one solitary figure.

Trevor scrambled over Janet to get out of the car. Her eyes fixedly probed the curled-up body from behind the window. I walked around from the driver's side. The motor was still running. Trevor stooped over the man. There was no turning back. My mind stopped racing with unanswerable questions. No longer a worried father or even a curious suburbanite, I was now simply a spectator. I was there and yet I wasn't. It was all in Trevor's hands. Janet and I were rapt observers at a private street-corner drama starring our son.

This was the quiet beginning of a thunderous change in our lives. But at that moment we were still a suburban family taking a quick peek at life in the raw before we rushed back to the safety of home.

"Here, sir, here's a blanket for you," Trevor offered as if

he were bringing a cup of coffee to a guest in his own dining room. He laid the crumpled, half-folded, yellow blanket on the man's arm.

The man sat up on his elbow, a dazed expression on his face, and mumbled, "Thank you very much. God bless you."

Trevor came back to me with a sober, businesslike expression on his face, and I handed him the pillow, feeling like his novice assistant. He carried the pillow to the man, and again the man repeated, "Thank you very much. God bless you."

Trevor simply returned the blessing, "God bless you," and turned back toward the car.

I spun around, relieved and about to burst with excitement. Janet turned down the car window warily and heard me blurt out: "Did you see his face? Did you see the smile on his face?" I was standing there announcing the event as though I were some kind of herald angel. Trevor, however, was calm.

After piling back into the car, we drove around the block and came back to see whether the man had unfolded our yellow blanket and placed Trevor's pillow under his head. We wanted to see him using our gifts, and we did. He looked as though he were at home sleeping, cuddled comfortably in a warm bed.

During the short trip home, we were inebriated with joy. "Did you see that smile?" I asked again and again.

"Yeah, it was great," Trevor concluded. He beamed.

Though Janet still had reservations about the wisdom of our excursion, she, too, was flooded with a rush of warm feelings. By the time we reached home, we felt as though we had returned from a religious experience. We felt as though we had been praying, but couldn't remember offering any words. I remember deciding we'd been praying with our actions.

Before going to bed, I stepped into the shower. With my

hand on the knob, I started to appreciate how amazing and nice it was just to turn a knob and feel warm water wash the cold and dirt away. The steam surrounding the faucet reminded me of the steam coming from that subway grate. Simple running water. Talk about taking things for granted! That night, and countless times since, I have felt gratitude for the ordinary things in life. I began to notice how snug my own bed was; how, at even the thought of food or a first twinge of hunger, I could satisfy my needs by walking to the refrigerator. These were lessons I thought I would teach my son. But I had to learn them first. We were all learning.

As he got ready for bed, Trevor thought about the man on the grate, now wrapped in the yellow blanket and resting his head on his pillow. Trevor fell asleep in no time at all, without a thought or desire for his other pillow.

On Friday evening, when I returned home as usual at exactly 5:20, Trevor met me at the front door. "Can we go again tonight? Mom and I found two more blankets."

I was annoyed at Trevor's badgering, because the next day was the most aggravating day of the week at work. Saturday was problem day for all the people who had bought home computers or video machines and wanted to know why they were having so much trouble getting what they wanted to come up on the screen. At the same time, I was curious. Did that man still have our blanket and pillow?

Thursday's experience had stuck with me all day. When I was tempted to complain about the pressures and demands of customers and problems, I flashed back to the scene at 15th and Moravian. I would see that unknown man's smile of gratitude, a man who had nothing. He brought perspective to my day-to-day difficulties. I guess I knew I would go again. Janet shared Trevor's excitement as he talked about going downtown. He had persuaded her all afternoon with his bantering and enthusiasm.

Finally, neither Janet nor I needed to weigh any pros or cons. All three of us wanted to go downtown again. We had two more blankets to give away and, besides, Friday had been a gloomy day with temperatures getting down to freezing. We looked forward to the warm reception we hoped awaited us. We wanted to see if that man was still sleeping under our blanket.

When we reached the grate, we were disappointed. He wasn't there. We drove on. A few blocks away we saw a different man wrapped tightly in our yellow blanket. We cheered. Our blanket was in circulation! But what had happened to that first man? We were getting our first glimpse of the hidden community, a veritable subculture operating out there on the streets.

As we cruised slowly past a doorway on Locust Street between 13th and Broad streets, Trevor shouted, "There's somebody!" Janet and I didn't see anyone. We drove around the block to show Trevor he was wrong, but sure enough, he'd spotted a half-hidden clump of humanity.

Even though it was only our second experience, we let Trevor venture out on his own. We had already decided there was no real danger. Something innocent and almost magical had pervaded Trevor's first encounter. We trusted that. Still, we parked a few feet from the shadowy doorway, as close as we could inch the wagon. The man did not stir. Trevor gently covered him, tucking the blanket around him. There was neither a nod nor a murmur.

From there, we continued down 13th Street to Walnut and on toward Rittenhouse Square. Trevor's eyes, riveted on the passing scene, spotted someone near a parking lot and some stores. "There's somebody walking." I stopped the car and followed Trevor, his arms bundled with a big blanket, as he strode toward a disheveled man who was shuffling along. We approached from behind, and the closer we got to him, the more the man picked up speed. As we tried to catch up with him, we were almost running.

Suddenly, the man wheeled around, reached in his pocket, and drew three black pens. He leveled them at us as if they were ray guns or hand-held bayonets poised to puncture our illusions of safety. Trevor jumped back in fear. I stopped short and reached for him. The man glared at us then rushed away. Trevor stated adamantly, "I don't want to try to help anyone who's up and walking around. No way! Never again."

Then and there we realized that you don't approach street people in any way that might be construed as threatening. In their lives, every stranger is a potential enemy. They must always look over their shoulders. They're human wanderers who never know if someone is going to kick them—or, occasionally, help them. I'd never noticed before that I expected people would be kind to me—even unknown people. I didn't know what it was to live in constant fear.

We drove a few blocks further and saw a man sitting cross-legged, looking vacantly into space. Trevor gave the bewildered man a blanket. As he chattered on the way home, he decided to nickname the man "Puzzle." Before we knew it, nicknames became the way we identified those we helped. We met them as people without names or identities. They seemed faceless. But as Trevor gave them names that reminded us of how we ran across them, we began to create some kind of personal link. The street people were becoming more than strangers in need of essential care and basic commodities. They were coming into focus as distinct personalities—members of a forgotten community.

As we drove home, we were all lost in our own thoughts and the glow of having helped two more people. We now had three blankets and one pillow in circulation on the streets of Philadelphia. On the surface, we were still a family crossing a dozen miles to the safety, warmth, and comfort of the suburbs. Yet already the breezes of transformation were rustling inside of us. And Trevor was leading the way.

2

Homeless in Suburbia

The brightly decorated streets of Philadelphia announced the coming of Christmas. We continued going downtown three or four nights a week. It all depended on Trevor. If he finished his homework, a trip downtown was his reward. We devised a regular route, where we could count on seeing about ten people—enough to deplete our nightly supply of blankets, coats, and sweaters.

One night, as we motored slowly in the inside lane near City Hall, Trevor spotted a grey-haired woman perched atop a wooden milk crate at the subway entrance on Broad near Chestnut. Nestled into the curved entryway of the brown marble office building adjacent to the subway entrance, she was settling in for the night. She'd chosen her resting place, appreciative of the warm air that drifted up the subway stairs. Holiday shoppers, arms laden with shopping bags full of shiny wrapped packages, hurried toward the homeward trains. Our woman patted her own shopping bags, haphazardly tied, one on each side of her like a fortress. The plastic bags held all her worldly goods.

We quickly double-parked amidst the angry stares, shaking fists, and complaining horns of the drivers who had to swing around us.

Trevor climbed out of the car, barely visible behind the bulky coat he had in his arms. Tonight we brought a special prize—Janet's old synthetic fur coat. We were parked by a skinny sidewalk tree that barely had branches enough to bear the twinkling white Christmas lights. Trevor handed the coat to the welcoming woman. She inspected the coat as if she were in Wanamaker's fine fur department. First she ran her hands along the shiny, textured fur. Then she examined the satiny lining, shoved her hands deep into the pockets, and stretched out the arms. Finally, she carefully folded the coat, smoothing its softness, and put it on her lap.

"Thank you, sweetheart," she said to Trevor with a gentle smile that extended up to her warm, squinty eyes.

"You're welcome," he nodded, and came back to the car, where he saw our delighted faces.

That old coat became the most wonderful gift we gave in that entire Christmas season. The woman's expression was constantly on our minds. The experience of giving with no thought of receiving anything but the joy on another's face reminded us of the reality of the true Christmas spirit—one that gives freely, purely for love of people.

We lingered for a moment, smiling at her, though she could hardly see us in the car. We saw a pronounced, broad grin spread across her face. She caressed her new treasure, our old coat. She almost looked as though she were waiting for someone special to pick her up to take her home for the holidays. But of course she wasn't waiting; she was just *there*. No impatience, no restlessness, no sense of anticipation. She was the picture of acceptance—she accepted the prospect of sleeping outdoors in freezing weather, her back pressed against the unyielding hardness of cold, brown marble.

Eventually, we learned that her name is June. She is from a family of twelve in North Carolina. Homeless four months before Trevor spotted her, she still won't talk much more about her circumstances. She sends one prevailing message—"Sufficient is the day . . ." She accepts her plight, always retaining a persistent, lingering smile.

Two nights later, when we saw June wearing Janet's old coat, we practically broke into elated applause and shouts of glee in the car. June had become special to all of us. She and Trevor shared a particular fondness. Whenever we went downtown, we searched for her.

One evening Trevor brought her a small transistor radio. They stood in "her" doorway, huddled close, turning the knobs and dials. Another evening, we went to a nearby store and bought her a hot chocolate and a piece of cake. When Trevor carried it to her, she crooned, "Thank you honey, do you want to share my cake with me?"

When I try to pinpoint what it was about June that captured our affection, I think it was her natural human pride, her graciousness. Her poise showed us just how important maintaining personal dignity can be on the streets.

Somewhere along the line we had decided to give away five dollars. As we discussed how much to allot to whom, June was at the top of our list. One dollar wasn't enough to really help; but five dollars would give it all away to one person, and was too much to ensure the person would buy food and not liquor. We decided to begin by giving June three dollars.

Trevor walked toward her, excited about the idea of giving June money and a choice of how to spend it on herself. Janet and I were waiting eagerly for her reaction and for that endearing smile. As we watched, we couldn't understand what we were seeing. She was shaking her head back and forth. Her hands would not take the money Trevor had in his outstretched hands.

Trevor shrugged as he returned to the car. "What happened?" we asked in unison.

"She said, 'Anything other than money.' "

We were puzzled, but we continued driving. Soon we saw a street person squatting on Walnut Street, his arms flailing. We learned later that the others on the street nicknamed him "Crazy." He would become enraged if approached—especially if you tried to give him anything. A well-meaning, well-dressed passerby was standing over "Crazy," having just given him money. "Crazy" grabbed the money, let loose a barrage of foul language, and flung it back at the man.

The wind blew the bills onto the sidewalk. One, two,

three dollars—the same amount we had offered June. We took it as a strong visual lesson: We weren't to give money.

Each experience fed the next one. Trevor's simple, direct determination to "go downtown and help them" was the only constant in our efforts. Everything else we were learning, night by night, person by person.

At home, the street people infiltrated our family consciousness in subtle ways. The extra, rarely worn sweaters and coats didn't seem important to keep for "just in case" or someday. The exhilaration of seeing June proudly sport her new coat had given us new motivation. Trevor's grandmother, who lives a few houses away, gave him two blankets when he told her that he wanted to help someone. When Liza, our teenage daughter, baked Christmas cookies to take downtown, June came into our conversation. These people were moving into our daily thoughts.

The answers to our questions about this completely new way of life came in tiny bits, occurrences, and unrelated pieces. When we took Liza's cookies downtown, we found out one place where street people get their food. Standing by a trash can, a man stood licking something that looked like creamed corn from his fingers as some of it ran down his tattered coat sleeve. His gooey hand accepted the cookies. As we watched Trevor deliver the cookies, he had no inkling of the feeling we had as we observed him blithely helping a hungry man as if he were doing something as simple as turning on the TV in his room. Something special was going on.

Later Trevor said, "They have to live on the streets, and right after you see one of them, you see somebody in a limousine pull up to a huge, empty mansion. It's such a difference. Some people can get anything they want, and these other people couldn't get a penny if they needed one."

We now saw street people as individuals, the way we saw our neighbors in Gladwyne. Closing our eyes became harder and harder. But we were running out of things to give.

The thought of going downtown empty-handed and seeing those people shivering was too painful.

I came home one evening to find that Trevor was taking matters into his own hands. He had urged Janet all day to find more clothes and blankets. She pointed out to him that there was nothing left. Finally, exasperated, she said, "Trevor, I can't find anything else to bring."

Trevor went back to his room, but soon returned with another one of his questions. "Why can't we ask people to help us?"

"How?" Janet asked. "By ringing doorbells?"

"I saw posters and signs at the shopping plaza," Trevor said. "Can we do something like that? We can put something up in Dad's store."

"OK, go and write something," Janet said, knowing that such an effort would keep Trevor busy—particularly since he was having such a tough time keeping up with his sixth-grade schoolwork in English composition.

She watched him walk to his room, glad to see him take the initiative to write something himself. He has dyslexia, and this reading disability makes school difficult for him. She often worried about how the evenings spent downtown would affect him. He was usually so uninterested in anything reminiscent of schoolwork.

By evening, Trevor had the basic version of his first public notice. Janet and I told him to go back and copy the words neatly and carefully on a piece of white paper. Then I had a thought. "Leave space in the right-hand corner and I'll put your picture there. I'll make photocopies on the machine in my store."

He began, "My name is Trevor," and reported in his unaffected way that we were bringing blankets to the street people of Philadelphia. He described June's face when we gave her Janet's coat, and promised we'd pick up donations if they couldn't be dropped off at my electronics store.

The response began gradually. A few coats or blankets

were left at the store, some neighbors called and stopped by. A customer who hadn't been in my store for several months spotted the notice in the window. She was a very proper matron from Philadelphia's wealthy Main Line suburbs. She said that if I would give her some copies of the notice, she would put them up in Bryn Mawr, a neighboring suburb.

An important—though unconscious—part of what we were doing was to offer the homeless that lived downtown some human contact, the feeling that someone cared about them. And it seemed to be contagious.

As the new donations filled our garage, Trevor rigged up a metal pole in the back of our newest anonymous contribution, a blue Volkswagen van. The keys had been given to us with a humble plea not to share the information as to who had supplied the vehicle. I hadn't expected this kind of response. Some current of compassion was being tapped—all because of Trevor's simple questions. We were amazed.

Onto the impromptu clothes rack went coats and jackets. We wanted to let people pick out what they wanted.

A festive spirit pervaded the night we first opened our traveling benevolence boutique. "Do you have anything in a 42 long?" one man joked. But we were surprised at how many things were tried on and rejected. The color was wrong. The material felt funny. It looked like a woman's. It was too heavy or too light.

Once we took one regular friend, Minnie, a selection of shoes; she barely had strips of cloth left covering her feet. "These are too shiny. I don't like patent leather." I was reminded of the old adage "Beggars can't be choosers." Indignantly, I realized that saying was completely false, like so much I had assumed about the poor. Although frustrating, the lesson that June had begun to teach us was reinforced: If the people on the streets dared to give up their dignity and some semblance of positive self-image, they'd cease to live. These people were survivors. They knew they were individuals capable of saying, "I'm me." They held fast to what they did and did not like.

Yet, from time to time, their reserve would give way. A street person would take Janet or me aside and awkwardly whisper a request for underwear. Another whispered request from the men was for cologne, as if they were ashamed of paying attention to the niceties as they clung to the shreds of their dignity.

No matter what resources we brought each night, it was the sight of little Trevor and his straightforward manner that captivated the street people. He didn't carry a lot of adult reserve along with him; he had no sense of judgment or condemnation. He had no fear. He could have been in his school yard greeting a classmate. He was open.

Because of the downtown ventures, Trevor increasingly began to show another quality: initiative. Out of nowhere, he asked his mother one afternoon after school: "Why don't we ask the *Main Line Times* to print our notice asking for blankets and clothes?"

"Oh, Trevor," Janet responded. "That's going too far. What do they care about what we're doing?"

But Trevor wouldn't stop, and Janet finally gave in. She drove him to the offices of our local weekly, but sat outside in the car, "too embarassed to go in." Trevor soon returned, announcing, "The lady said she's really interested and she's going to call and she'd like to come down with me some time."

By accident or perhaps by providence, Trevor was referred to a young reporter, Susan Greenspon, who had joined the weekly paper during the same week we had begun our downtown trips. Enthusiastic and eager, she decided to write a feature story, though—as we discovered later—she had to use heavy persuasion to convince the editor that the story was worthy. Susan did come along with us on a trip downtown, and brought along an extra plaid-lined coat.

Things were never the same after her article and photograph appeared in the local paper on December 29, 1983. Channel 10, Philadelphia, came first. Then it was Channel 6, Channel 3, the Philadelphia newspapers, the *New York Times*, the wire services. The Philadelphia City Council placed its official stamp of approval on our nightly treks with a formal resolution. In less than a month after our first trip downtown, the entire country was reading about Trevor.

We were uncomfortable with the publicity, but it paled alongside the responses we were getting from the people themselves: the appreciative eyes; the sudden smile on an unshaven face; the direct, heartfelt thank you; the staunch dignity that held up in the face of lonely nights sleeping on the streets; the warm greetings on cold nights. One evening, late in December, Trevor gave a special surprise gift to two elderly men, Chuck and George, who were sitting on milk crates sharing a cup of soup, passing one single paper container back and forth. As we drove away, Chuck waved and called out, "Have a Happy New Year everyone!" I'm certain that they didn't observe another year's passing with a gala party, but their appreciation for living through twelve more months was obvious.

Each evening we went downtown it became more likely that we would return the next night. The experience was exhilarating. We wanted to repeat it—it was as if we were feeding a habit. Without realizing it, we had become addicted. Our lives were becoming centered on these downtown trips, and everything else was fading into the background.

The publicity that Susan's article generated resulted in checks, cash, and donations from an amazing variety of sources. Each one seemed to take us by surprise, each one motivated us to go on. People couldn't resist responding. One Sunday a friend, a fellow parishioner, pressed a blank envelope into my hand as we greeted each other with a handshake. He leaned over and whispered, "Let's keep this between you and me, Frank." He repeated this two other Sundays. Each envelope contained a check for $1,000.

Once when we were illegally parked, stopped to fill plates, I saw a policeman striding with authority toward us. "Oh, oh," I warned Janet. "This time we're going to get a ticket." I watched the policeman reach into his coat pocket. But instead of a traffic ticket, he handed me a five-dollar bill and said, "God bless you. Keep up the good work."

By March, we were going downtown nightly. We felt guilty if we didn't go. On many nights, we'd say, "Let's not go in tonight . . . I don't feel like going in . . . We can miss one night, can't we?" Invariably, however, we'd load up the van because we realized the street people were expecting us and we felt uncomfortable letting them down. No matter how reluctant we might have been to leave home on a particular night, we always went home satisfied inside. Never before had the Bible verse "Tis more blessed to give than to receive" meant so much.

We were receiving much more than we were giving, and it was the same for our growing group of volunteers. Repeatedly, they *thanked* us for the chance to give to others.

Just as the contributions came from a variety of sources, so too did the volunteers appear in sundry shapes and sizes. I remember one young, dark-haired woman in particular. She had a pensive wariness in her hazel eyes when she rang our doorbell, which she did nearly every night, week after week. She was aloof, reluctant to talk, and she refused to come downtown. Dropping her grocery bag full of peanut butter and jelly sandwiches, she hastened to her silver sedan and sped away.

Janet worried about her; I wondered what her motivation was. Something spurred her to come, but what?

One night, Janet took her aside and asked her if she would like to see the people she was helping to feed. Just ride in the van, she didn't have to get out.

Tears welled up and then streamed down her face as she unsuccessfully tried to blink away her obvious pain. Finally, she said, "My father is an alcoholic who has been on the streets for years." The sandwiches allowed her to demonstrate, in a tangible way, the love she had for a man long lost and given up by the rest of the family.

Who were the street people? This question, in my mind that first December night, began to find an answer. They had families, at least some did. I kept looking into the older men's faces that night wondering if, just maybe, the woman's sandwiches had reached her father. I hoped against realistic hope that they had.

The momentum was carrying us forward. We saw no way of stopping. We didn't want to stop. We were changing and we could not change back.

The depth of the changes hit me as I rummaged through the garage on a rare quiet Saturday. I picked up a cloth laying on a workbench and inhaled its scent. Ah, those dark leather seats. It had been a long time since I had thought of my "toy," my 1958 Rolls Royce. The craftsmanship of that automobile was impeccable, a mechanical diamond. How I had waxed and polished that car! I'd sold it only a few months ago; but as I looked out at the worn wagon and the well-used van in the driveway, that Rolls seemed eons past in my life. The van's doors were open. I could see a ladle on the seat, and chili stains on the step from last night. I quietly refolded the cloth and put it in a box with the other rags. Those days were gone.

We were rapidly drifting away from the friendly, familiar setting of Main Line suburbia. We were becoming aliens, as different from our neighbors as we had thought the street people were from us. Trevor already felt the effects at school. When his classmates discovered his downtown visits, they taunted him. "Hey, Trevor, got a blanket for me?" Trevor responded appropriately, "If I see you on 8th and Walnut, I'll be glad to give you one." Some boys had hit him at recess in the school yard, and he was hurting on the inside too. He felt like an outsider. He never told us in those first months, but he would sometimes go quietly to his room and cry.

The immense change in our lives came home to Janet and me one evening at a dinner party with our church group. We had spent the previous year together, weekly discussing and reading the Bible and ways to bring it into our lives. These were our friends, the people we felt most comfortable with—people who shared our concerns about family, church, and country. On that particular evening we were accompanied by Mark, a young Hollywood director and a volunteer Christian youth minister. He was visiting us as a prelude to discussing a movie on the story of Trevor's past few months.

In the course of the dinner, whenever references came up about Trevor, they clattered into the conversation like a knife hitting the floor. A polite, restrained nod, or "How nice," and the conversation would quickly veer to the country club, plans for summer vacation . . . "What was your golf score today?" . . . "Are you going to Martha's Vineyard again this summer?" . . . "I heard that your daughter was accepted into Penn. That's wonderful."

After dinner as everyone went into the formal living room to continue the conversation, Janet, Mark, and I drifted away into the kitchen. We were there alone, standing near the refrigerator, when Mark asked, "Do you realize what's happening here?"

Yes, we did.

Janet and I suddenly felt very alone, separated, unconnected. We realized that we had become "socially" homeless in suburbia. What mattered to our friends and neighbors no longer mattered to us. We carried images in our heads of men and women sleeping on grates, on subway steps, in doorways, and in alleys. What mattered to us, what had become the focus of our lives, hovered at the extreme edges of our friends' lives—far away and downtown.

We wanted to let them in on the passion of our experiences. I wanted to yell, "Look, we sat together all last year with our Bibles open. We had a good time sharing what we read together. We used to love those moments. Talking about Jesus going to the well, about the Good Samaritan, about helping our neighbor, about loving others. But is that enough? I know it isn't anymore." How I wanted them to see June's smile—to experience the magic of helping another human being keep warm and finding your own heart wrapped in the kindnesses returned.

Something had happened to us. We could never be the same. It was as though Janet, Trevor, and I were in a bubble, all by ourselves. Cut off. Over there in that living room were all the other people we once felt a part of. Once, but no more.

Now I had a different feeling. I felt closer to the Lord. A few days after the dinner party Janet confirmed that she had the same feeling. It was a Saturday evening, several months after the first trip downtown. As we filled thermoses and stirred the stew, she said it for herself and for Trevor and for me: "How different we have become!" The silence confirmed it.

3

The Sorry Kingdom

Once Janet and I admitted to ourselves that our lives and priorities had changed, I began to think back over the numerous times we'd loaded the van, turned the ignition key, and headed downtown. I wasn't sure what had occurred to subtly transform us. Was there an event or two that initiated these changes? Bits and pieces of the last several months resurfaced from my memory in the weeks following the dinner party. Then one afternoon, I slumped down comfortably into the floral loveseat in the den, determined to let the events of the past months play across my mind in order to teach me. With my eyes closed the vivid images overtook me. . . .

The bristled, whiskered sneer of a black man leered inches from my face outside the car window. I clutched the steering wheel as my stomach turned over. It was after eight o'clock in the evening. I glanced in front of the van; all I saw was a deserted street. Nothing was visible in the rearview mirror. The winter-gray emptiness of city sidewalks prevailed.

Out of the passenger window I caught a glimpse of a rainbow-striped hat worn by another man who was standing on the sidewalk. He was bent over, listening to Trevor. Another shadowy figure, with arms defiantly crossed, lurked behind him. My heart stopped. What if this were a ploy? Was the man at my window a decoy of some sort? A distraction to keep me from focusing on Trevor? Janet's eyes were riveted on our son. Anger began to rise inside of me. We were trying to help these people. Their suspicion infuriated me. If they tried to hurt my son. . . .

I turned to stammer an explanation to the face pressed against my window. He wanted to know what we were doing in his part of town. "We've been bringing blankets and clothes downtown . . . some food, uh, for about a month. My son," I pointed across the van toward Trevor, "he saw a report on TV; he wanted to do something to help."

The tall man with Trevor straightened to his full height. "Cool it, man," he said with authority to the challenger beside me. He then looked down at Trevor and smiled, his face aglow with a welcoming smile. I was startled to see how foreign to the tension and suspicion of the last few moments his expression was. "It's great meetin' you," the man said. And that is how Alex, a self-acclaimed prince of the streets in paint-splattered overalls, became our first real instructor of life on the streets.

Just minutes before, Alex's suspicious companion (whom we later named "Old Deuteronomy" because he was a cryptic philosopher) and two others sat enfolded in the warm fragrant air that filtered up from the building's laundry room below their grate. With their backs propped against the old brick building, legs straight in front of them, they laid claim to the corner of Van Pelt and Chestnut as their territory.

Trevor had initiated this confrontation by invading their space, bearing shoeboxes full of peanut butter and jelly sandwiches, cupcakes, and juice. The talk of blankets had brought three of the four to the side door toward the van. The other remained slumped on a flattened cardboard box. Both of his legs were broken.

Alex, we came to recognize, sometimes lapsed into a mystery world. After one disappearance, when asked where he'd been, he replied, "I've been holding the planet together." In that moment, strange as it may seem, he had been somehow almost believable.

Alex, the average bum to mainstream society, was considered a noble musician and dreamer in his kingdom of the streets. His friends always recognized his presence and re-marked on his absence. He often filled the trash-strewn crevices and frozen air with haunting melodies from his plaintive flute as he sauntered and swayed through his small empire. He embodied a paradox of dignity, beauty, and despair among the ashes and rot. What a tragic prince— a noble pauper.

From that first meeting and after, the aroma of cheap, pungent cologne brought Alex to my thoughts. Alex wore a strong fragrance. Even if he rarely bathed, his multicolored hat and odd concern for appearance evidenced his struggle to retain his personal pride. He was *somebody*. A distinctive, and somewhat disconnected, person. His uniqueness, his wonderful smile, his wanderings and delusions raised ques-tion after question each time we saw him.

Up until this point, I had thought that my role in these mid-city jaunts was to help my son learn compassion first-hand. But Alex was a man, a person I didn't understand even though I wanted to. It was all so confusing and yet, I had to admit, strangely compelling.

As I worked at the shop, my thoughts kept sneaking downtown. My fingers separated electrical wires and pro-cessed receipts, but my mind drifted among the people of the city streets I'd traveled all of my life and yet had never really known or experienced. My preoccupation was remi-niscent of the first year I started my business. The work con-sumed me. No matter where I was, the business permeated everything. I even saw TV screens and customers in my sleep.

But what was happening to me now? Helping Trevor de-liver care packages or scooping up a ladleful of steaming vegetable soup and emptying it into a styrofoam cup, only to hand it to a woman who mumbled incoherently—these times brought a sense of accomplishment that no other task duplicated. I began to realize that the first trip downtown and its aftermath were shifting my life's direction and priorities. These ragged people, smelly and alien, were affecting my business, without ever crossing the threshold into my shop.

I had experienced something revolutionary. It was the invigorating feeling of being close to somebody; somebody I'd never seen before, somebody completely different from myself. I was hooked on the simple giving that, when received, is given back in the matchless human reward of knowing a person would make it through one more day.

To know we were needed and were supplying someone with affection—letting them know that Trevor cared, our family cared, and that I cared exhilarated me. Twenty cups of coffee couldn't reproduce the nervous energy and the lightheadedness that I felt in those unplanned moments when it became irrelevant who was the giver and who was the recipient. A very human exchange was moving inside of us all. I felt something that I can only describe as sacramental. Something as spiritual as a church service.

I had reminded myself repeatedly, as did Janet, that this was crazy. All we were doing, as one person sarcastically put it, was "bandaging a few scrapes on terminally ill and bleeding people." While my internal argument went on, the efforts grew and grew.

Winter was waning. The snow disappeared. A few of the street people came to our church to tell the suburban, white, affluent church members who they were and how they survived. Both sides wore protective masks. The congregation brought masks of caution and propriety; the street people wore visages of toughness and rage. Both masked fear of those unknown to their way of life. After the first man spoke of his morning prayers lifted up each morning from a cubbyhole in an alleyway, the masks began to crumble. Honesty broke through and God's presence came into the sanctuary. Hesitant but friendly greetings were offered by both sides. A paper was sent around requesting helpers to cook. Last week, where only six signatures were registered, this week there were seventy. A few of the church people began to venture downtown with us when they could. Each morsel of food became precious. A hundred or more street people appeared out of nowhere each night as the blue van wound through the not-so-deserted streets on its regular route.

No matter who we met or who was with us helping, each night we heard the same things. "Got a burger?" "Got a burger?" The annoying phrase resounded every evening between six and nine. The donated McDonalds hamburgers were the first to go. "Where's the corn?" "I don't want rice." "Don't like yogurt." The complaints and questions echoed down the line. When one would ask, they all would ask. Sometimes it was awful. The smell of cooked food and dirty bodies in the warming weather could be nauseating. As the humid summer and ever-increasing crowds approached, we all longed for the intimacy of the winter when one cold, homeless man sleeping on a subway grate had said "God bless you" to a little boy.

And yet, when just one too many full plates had been ungratefully thrown down on the pavement after only a few stops, and we knew we had a multitude with growling stomachs waiting within blocks and there would be nothing left, that special holy moment of giving would recur.

One such night we turned the motor off at the park, our last stop. A Hispanic fellow walked up to the van. Janet shook her head with a tight-lipped smile. "We're out, sorry." He gestured that it didn't matter. He spoke gently, "Let me thank you for all of this." With his hands clutched to his chest, he turned and walked away. We would come back again. That man had just guaranteed it.

We still had more to learn about these people we spent our evenings with. They were so unpredictable. Sometimes these pathetic people became master teachers in the ultimate meaning of life, because they knew what it was to barely hang on. Stripped of everything but the right to breathe and laugh, they spoke of the elemental side of life—the important things.

But then there were times when these people seemed to fit all of the stereotypes I used to believe. Some were lazy and ungrateful, some were crazy and uncivilized. Others were belligerent and unresponsive. Some were ultimate cons—experts at manipulation and deceit.

That night as the van rumbled home, I thought about the two sides I had seen on the streets. It had been a difficult night. A fight had broken out. There was a woman with three kids at the last stop, and we were out of food. Just the stop before some guy had taken a huge plateful of food, spit on it, and hurled it to the gutter with a snarling remark. I said, "If they were like us, they wouldn't be here." A simple phrase—but it was the key that began to unlock the closed door of my understanding of the homeless.

I straightened from my reverie and mumbled aloud, "If they were like us, they wouldn't be here." I was in my lovely home and they were on the streets; yet I was becoming a stranger in my own neighborhood. I, Frank Ferrell, had changed from being a father who had acted out of responsibility and compassion, to a person who cared *why* people lived in despair and poverty. I'd changed because I had met too many paradoxical people, full of both strength and inner decay. Janet, Trevor, and I had seen too much. The lives we'd lived and understood for years hadn't told us the full story on what life was really about.

Now it was time to find out why these street people, my friends, existed on the streets. I needed to discover what I could about how and why Alex had become a prince of the streets, and all the others members of such a sorry kingdom.

4
Empty Houses

I pushed aside the stack of newspapers on the coffee table. Scanning headlines for articles on homelessness could wait for another day. This morning, onto the small cleared space, I dropped the March 26, 1984 issue of *People* magazine I had rushed out to buy at the first ray of morning from the local newsstand near the Gladwyne Village Shopping Area. Skipping the contents page, I rifled through the pages. Page 60: There it was. The headline read, "Philadelphia's Street People Have Found a Ministering Angel in Tiny Trevor Ferrell."

Halfway into the first paragraph the phone rang, and I heard Janet's voice from the kitchen. "Frank, will you get that?" I stuffed the magazine into my already bulging leather portfolio. Reading it would have to wait along with the other tattered and yellowing articles and clippings sticking out of the mishmash of file folders. I picked up the telephone receiver with a sigh.

Another week was in full swing. Each day sped by. The frenzied pace to get to work, shuttle the kids to school or to friends' houses, and still find time to go downtown to the streets each evening never seemed to end. My dedication to finding out why Alex and the others were on the streets had not waned. As the weeks passed, I began to come to grips with the truth about myself. I naturally acted on the basis of intuitive impulse. I preferred to find a job and do it. I could figure out how to fix most anything by jumping in and beginning. My business depended on my ability to look at a broken machine and make it work again. Trevor is like that too. He saw the people in need and wanted to act immediately.

Just as Trevor's schoolwork was a chore for him, I found studying homelessness a demanding discipline. Neither of us found reading easy. Each word was a painstaking struggle that had to be endured. I knew I had to read and hear what others had learned through firsthand experience and research so that we could avoid some of the common mistakes and problems. So I did read. But no matter how determined I was, the street people themselves were the teachers whose very lives and words explained the most relevant truths of how one faces a life on the streets.

Take Sonny, for instance. He knew the streets like the back of his hand. So, too, he knew the people. His normal greeting was, "Hi there! Sonny's still number one!" He loved to call himself by his first name. Except for his boisterous greetings, he kept quiet and to himself. He was a loner.

One night when I picked him up in the van to take him across town, I looked closely at the oil-stained pillow he carried under his arm. I recognized the pillowcase. Trevor had given it to him weeks ago. As we rode, he told me he had been a cabinet builder and was the father of three. His family lived across the river in New Jersey. He hated photographers and never allowed his picture to be taken. Although he didn't say so, I knew he was terrified of the thought that his family would find out his condition. Every year, at Thanksgiving, his father would come to Philadelphia to visit. Sonny saved and bartered enough money each fall to dress himself respectably, pay for an expensive dinner for two, and send his dad back to a hotel in a taxi that would stop first and drop Sonny off in front of a staid-looking apartment building. A tenderhearted tenant annually lent him a key to the lobby door so that his charade would convince even the most suspicious of parents.

And what was it that kept Sonny in this predicament, pretending year after year? The information I read in document after document attributed cases like Sonny's to substance abuse. Sonny called it booze. He lost his wife and kids and job because of the bottle, and now it was the only thing that was stable in his life. He knew how to deaden the sheer horror, meaninglessness, and disconnectedness of his life. Eating and sleeping were irrelevant. His consuming craving for alcohol was typical of others we met, whose central focus had become liquor or some other addictive drug.

When the van arrived each night, Sonny waited until everyone else was served. He didn't much care if there would be food for him or not. He came to see Trevor. The mahogany rosary Sonny gave to him soon after they met still hangs over Trevor's bed.

One night as we delivered food, a feverish and nauseated Trevor wanted to stay in the van. He was in pain and uncharacteristically withdrawn. Sonny repeatedly inquired, "Where's Trevor?" as he nudged past each volunteer. Arriving at the van door he spotted Trevor huddled in the middle seat. With an intense expression and a shaky, pointed finger, the alcoholic promised, "I'm going to pray for you. I'm going to get everybody to pray for you." That night I had to carry Trevor to his bed.

The next evening at the same corner, a cheer sounded when Trevor stepped down from the van. Sonny, the first to hug Trevor, proudly claimed, "We prayed for you, Trevor." Tears filled his eyes, and he quickly faded into the back of the exuberant group. Trevor followed him, elbowing his way through the long line of those waiting to be fed. When he reached him, he pleaded somberly, "Sonny, don't drink too much tonight." The older man zipped up Trevor's jacket to make sure he wasn't cold. "It's just that way, kid. It happens." Sonny left Trevor and walked up to me. "Frank, I want you to have this." He reached into the pocket of his lined army coat and dropped a tarnished bronze military service medal in my hand. The red, white, and blue cloth was soiled and worn from much handling. "Great kid," he nodded in Trevor's direction. "Sonny'll see you tomorrow."

Alcohol was the primary reason Sonny inhabited a cardboard-lined doorway within a block of Claus Oldenburg's shiny "Clothespin" statue in city center. Sonny's broken family ties and a jobless veteran status also contributed to his homelessness, as is frequently the case. Whether booze was the cause, effect, or response to family, work, and civilian readjustment problems, who knows? The booze just helps Sonny quit hurting. When he quits drinking, he says, he realizes he doesn't have any place to go or anyone who cares. So he drinks. That's survival for him.

Alcoholism and drug abuse are fairly obvious reasons people become homeless drifters, but they're not the only ones. Carlos and Juan are good examples. Neither is a junkie or wino, but they call the streets home. Jobless, inexperienced, and from the "wrong" ethnic group, they grew up poor boys in the projects. Now they find the city of their birth inhospitable.

One Saturday night, the two Hispanic cousins—or so they called themselves—sauntered up to the van, trying to restrain their bursting excitement. Juan beamed as he asked Trevor to find something to write on. "Gotta draw a map for you," Carlos whispered loudly. Continuing to pour punch, I watched the two young men gesture and talk animatedly as they drew their lines on a brown paper lunch bag. Janet and Trevor huddled with them over the hood of the van.

"What was that all about?" I asked Trevor after goodbyes were exchanged and we were rumbling on down Maple Street. Trevor leaned up toward the driver's seat and excitedly said, "Carlos and Juan just built a new house under the Girard Avenue Bridge. They dug trenches and stuck pieces of heavy cardboard up for walls." Janet chimed in, "And they spread clear plastic tarp on the floors for carpet and covered the window holes so that they can see out."

My wife and son filled in all of the details. "We promised to go visit them next week, right Mom?" Janet nodded, "If we can find it and get under the bridge without breaking our necks."

The astounding ingenuity of the pair made me wonder anew why they were forced to resort to refrigerator boxes and used painter's plastic to fashion a shelter for themselves. They were the flesh-and-bone people described in a recent *New York Times* survey a friend gave me to read. It declared that young, unskilled men from the city's ghettoes and projects were the fastest-growing population among the homeless. Carlos and Juan weren't transient hoboes drifting from place to place at random. They had both lived all their lives in Philly's projects and attended Philly's high schools. Devoid of any marketable skills, Carlos never located work outside of a few odd jobs. Juan had served as a short-order cook for a café until it closed its doors. Unable to find jobs in an economy where even the vocationally trained compete heavily to overcome barrier after barrier to long-term employment and job security, the unskilled skid to the ranks of the uncountable masses on the streets.

Even having family nearby is of little help. The children, elderly relatives, and income earners barely fit into the communal dwelling places, or low-income housing apartments, that are often stretched beyond normal limits. Poverty pushes the young and strong who have come of age out of the nest to fend for themselves. Now that Carlos and Juan have a fairly warm and semidry place to live, maybe they can spend more time looking for work instead of a place to lay their heads. But it's hard to enroll in a city college or apply for a job when your address is "under the Girard Avenue bridge." Job interview call-backs are impossible when the nearest pay phone is four blocks east and one block south of the bridge.

Meanwhile, no one includes Carlos or Juan in unemployment or census statistics. Their neighbors in abandoned cars, subway tunnels, and empty warehouses join them in the ranks of anonymous Americans. Somehow, the creativity that is left in them refuses to succumb to the reality of not existing within society. They just take their ingenuity underground and build cardboard castles under dirty bridges and call the place "home."

I began to see that Carlos and Juan, as well as Sonny, had potential to build a life somewhere other than on the concrete of city sidewalks. Sonny needed help dealing with alcohol and the factors that led to his addiction. Carlos and Juan needed a mailing address and vocational training. Mostly, all three needed time and consistent encouragement, a warm, dry bed, and good food. They all could probably leave the streets permanently.

Yet others, like June, will never function outside of their haphazard way of life without a full miracle or assistance for the rest of their days. June reports that she worked for the Social Security Administration. She seriously claims it was her job to "redirect the A bomb." Sleeping in city shelters, parks, train stations, ventilation grates, and doorways is rarely a choice for those like June. Anywhere from one-half to one-third of street people share her plight: They are mentally ill.

As I dug through the pile of articles on the coffee table, I kept seeing a key phrase: "The de-institutionalization era." This referred to a swing in mental health policy that burgeoned in the late 1960s and continued for a decade. Hundreds of thousands of institutionalized patients were released with the hope that the newly discovered tranquilizing drugs would give these people back their independence. One source declared that mental hospitals dropped over 400,000 patients from their rolls between 1955 and 1982.

Promised community mental health facilities and programs to help those who had been released were never actualized. Empty promises were swept away and forgotten during federal administration turnovers. Less than one-quarter of all the patients discharged remained in any kind of program. Meanwhile, a generous portion of the remaining 300,000 people, many of whom were never heard from again, walked out into the streets with no homes, no jobs, and no support. They've been left alone to live lives of quirky habits and muddled ideas.

June, for example, hoards scraps of clean, white paper. A dropped ballpoint pen or a pencil stub is a luxury. For hours on end she hunches over a paper spread smoothly over the piece of cardboard on her lap and draws stick figures from left to right across the page.

One late afternoon as spring approached, Janet said to June, "Did you sleep last night? You look tired." The brim of June's brown velvet cap wobbled as she shook her head from side to side. "No, ma'am, not much. Betty was yellin' all night."

"Who's Betty? A friend of yours?" June stopped and looked at Janet quizzically, as if she should've already known Betty's identity, then replied, "No, Mrs. Ferrell, Betty is one of the voices in my head. She's the most regular at night. She always yells."

June's past is nearly a mystery. She appears to be a Southerner in her late sixties. Though she says she's one of seven children, no one apparently knows, or cares, where she is.

There are telltale signs that June was once institutionalized. References to "her ward" and "group time" seem to point to familiarity with a structured, clinical way of life. She talks about politicians and doctors with the same distrust. "They don't want to help an old lady like me. Ain't got no money, never did, never will."

Harmless and sweet, June loves to dress up and carry a different handbag or sport a new style of hat each day. Her shopping bags are full of dress-up items. The thought of reinstitutionalizing June doesn't ring true as the most helpful thing for her. She needs constant love and security and a place to belong in her last years.

An agency might be able to help her with some immediate needs, but my research and phone calls showed me that the existing community services and benevolent ministries, however good they might be, were just a hopeful drop in the staggering downpour of need we were just beginning to encounter. Some things agencies can't provide. Not even the most well-intentioned nine-to-five worker behind a desk can supply family backing, supportive community, and permanent supervised housing for everyone that comes in need.

The recurring advice on how to help the homeless I continued to come across was confirmed by what I saw on our nightly runs. June, and thousands like her across the nation, needed aid to locate a place to stay where compassionate people could supervise and love her. Left alone to her delusions, she will never recover. Given love and acceptance, and a place to call her own, my studies and my inner hunches say she may be able to regain a sense of self strong enough to begin to unravel what is real from what is not in her tangled web of memories.

The mentally ill cry out for a special type of caring advocacy, but clearheaded Mitch needs a home too. He knows the reality of his life and position. He's not crazy, just handicapped. His story rips my heart apart each time I think of it. A victim of cerebral palsy, Mitch can barely articulate a word clearly enough for a stranger to understand. Only with time can his speech be deciphered. He shuffles and struggles behind his metal walker with plastic hand grips, blackened by subway soot and city grime.

Mitch, a man in his fifties, makes his home in a subway entrance. He is the filthiest human I've ever seen. He owns only what he wears on his back; his plaid flannel shirt is no longer soft. A crust of grime covers his unlaundered clothes. His hands are mottled gray with ground-in dust.

Mitch doesn't go anywhere during the day for food. He can't manage his walker for very long. Each night we stop to carry in the most laden plate we can fill. We intentionally keep aside a couple of fast food hamburgers to stuff silently into his coat pockets for whenever he might get hungry before our next trip downtown.

On one winter run, Mitch didn't come out to greet the vanload of people and receive his dinner as he usually did. Janet and I went into the subway entrance to find him. Collapsed in a corner, our gray-haired friend breathed noisily as he slept. His walker wasn't beside him. With a quick glance down the stairs, we located it: shoved on its side in a hallway corner. As I started down the rigid cement steps to retrieve it, Janet gently tapped Mitch's shoulder. "What happened?" she asked. "Kids," Mitch slurred, and blinked with sleepy eyes. "Punks, they kicked me. Hit me with the walker. Pushed me down the stairs. Threw the walker after me."

As he straightened up a little, the bruises on his hands became obvious. "Your hands, Mitch. Why are they so bruised?" "Kids stepped on them. I climb up a step; they stomp on me," he answered. Mitch looked down at his hands and then at Janet. "Don't worry. They'll heal." By this time I had the walker in hand and was nearly at the top of the stairs. "How'd you get back up here?" I asked, not sure if I was ready to hear any more. "Two men carried me," was his garbled reply. At least there's a tiny speck of generosity in this mad world, I thought wryly.

I returned to the van and asked Trevor to bring in the food. Janet stayed by his side. "Want us to take you to the hospital?" she asked. "No," Mitch said. "No insurance, nothing they can do."

Sadly, we knew he was right. Even if he spent the night in the hospital, he'd be released in a day or two with bills he couldn't pay. He'd be right back here. As inhumane as it was, the subway entrance was the place he knew best.

On our way home that night, anger at such pitiful injustice and violence burned inside of me. "Good God Almighty," I ranted in my prayers, "why on earth does this craziness continue? Mitch can't even walk. Where is his family or his friends? How can they leave him out there? Why does he hang on? Why doesn't he just give up and die? I don't understand." I was too restless and fitful to sleep that night.

A few nights later we drove past a block of abandoned buildings on 9th Street. Trevor, riding beside me, wiped off a circle of fog from the passenger window and peered out. He broke the silence. "Look at all these empty houses. Why should people be living on the streets when there are these houses that are already built with no one living in them? Why can't we get one of these empty places for the street people?"

I thought of all the people we had seen that night. I especially thought of Charlene, whom we had met for the first time. This tiny woman, born with no arms, had her two children living with her on the streets. She couldn't even hold the baby. They weren't the first family we'd encountered. Evicted, jobless, and handicapped, with no address for welfare checks to be sent to, her growing brood existed by going to drop-in shelters, to rescue missions, to the Ferrell family van. Charlene and each of our friends on the streets survived in a sorry state, regardless of the differing reasons that propelled them there.

Alcohol, drugs, broken families, poverty, lack of job skills, mental illness, physical handicaps, inhibited social abilities . . . the reasons I discovered were far more complicated than I suspected when I decided to explore the whys of homelessness. Tragically, many of the events leading to this exposed means of barest survival were not the sole result of the individual's choices.

I wished we had a roof to put over all of their heads so that some semblance of peace and security would be available should they choose to take advantage of it. I was discovering that the rootlessness of the streets, be it experienced for a few days or many years, has a similar effect on all: It leaves each person brutalized physically, spiritually, and emotionally. Trevor was right. We needed to find a home for the homeless.

But planning how to make a dream of housing the homeless come true was not on the agenda for that particular Saturday evening. We ran out of food before the last stop and had to turn away scores of people. I went home overwhelmed, and the idea of housing the homeless was momentarily buried beneath all of the immediate needs.

The next morning the family struggled out of bed, all six of us scrambling to get ready at the same time. We rushed to church. Jody joined the other children her age in Children's Church. Liza and Allen found friends to sit with. Janet, Trevor, and I dropped into a pew as the choir began to sing. I opened my bulletin and scanned the morning's order of service. I stopped short, blinked my eyes, and looked again. Slowly turning toward Janet, I found her already turned toward me. I smiled hesitantly, "Do you see what I see?" She nodded, and squeezed her eyes to stop the tears.

The day's sermon title was "Empty Houses." After the message concluded, we were asked to sing a closing hymn, "Lord Speak to Me." As I flipped through the pages to find the hymn on page 399, I knew I'd already been spoken to.

We could not guess how it would happen, but we'd been shown a sign—a directional signal. An empty house was out there somewhere in Philadelphia, waiting for us. It was our task to find it. For the sake of Sonny, Carlos, Juan and the rest, we had to obey. We were to find a place that our new friends could call home in the middle of the inner city.

5

Trevor's Place—A Home for the Homeless

Poplar Street in North Philadelphia was cold, windy, and empty on the morning in March when I nervously pushed an old key into the dark green door of a deserted thirty-three-room brick hotel next to Mill's one-story shop for generators and starters. I had been elated while driving along the Schuylkill Expressway from Gladwyne, then stunned by reality as I motored along Poplar Street. The attractive row homes along the expressway had changed into burned-out store fronts, overgrown empty lots, and rusty abandoned cars as I neared my destination, number 1618.

Father Domenic Rossi, a Catholic priest of the Norbertine order, was waiting for me when I arrived, on hand to share what he knew about housing the homeless. The boyish-looking priest was as impatient as I was to see whether we had a white elephant on our hands, or if our dreams were about to be realized.

I kept thinking, "This is too good to be true." I fiddled with the key, the lock, the door, feeling clumsy as well as uncertain. First the key was upside down, then the tumblers in the lock refused to budge. Father Rossi seemed on the verge of helping me when the door gave way. As I stepped inside, I faced a stairway going upstairs. I didn't know which way to go. I had never done this before. Where and how do you inspect a hotel that someone wants to give you as a home for the homeless?

Just days before, following the confirming Sunday service, we had entered into discussions about housing the homeless with other members of the Gladwyne Presbyterian church. The members of the Outreach Group encouraged us to consider the St. Francis Residence in New York City as a model for a home in Philadelphia. Other church friends offered their help and assistance. All we needed was the building.

Then a late-afternoon phone call interrupted our worries. "Peace, Mr. Ferrell," the woman's voice on the other end of the line greeted. "This is Miss Darling from the Peace Mission Movement. Mother Divine wishes to speak with you." The phone clicked and then an articulate and animated voice proceeded to tell me that a thirty-three-room hotel with nineteen bathrooms was ours if we wanted it. "The building certainly isn't a showplace or up to our normal standards. We used the facility as a rooming house at one time, and it has stood empty for at least three years. But it is yours if you can use it!" Mother Divine, the current leader of the movement and widow of the founder, Father Divine, had read about Trevor and had seen the television reports of our downtown visits. She explained that the spirit of Trevor's actions exemplified what the Peace Mission existed for.

Janet and I knew Mother Divine from visits and special banquets we attended at various Peace Mission Churches in the metropolitan area and at Woodmont, the seventy-three-acre estate the mission occupied in Gladwyne. Founded fifty years ago, the movement's followers are scattered throughout the country and the world. Trevor had visited the Woodmont grounds with us and with his schoolmates a few times in the past few years. Yet we never dreamed the mission would donate a building to us, let alone this one at 1618 Poplar Street.

Now, inside of that very building, I hesitated. Where should I begin? Father Rossi led the way, and we walked through the reception room on the left, back to a non-functioning kitchen and through a dirty tiled hallway, until we'd gone full circle to a second living area to the right of the entrance. Each of the rooms facing onto Poplar Street had a large picture window; through dirty, broken venetian blinds I could see the battered and worn-out two-story houses across the street. My friends on the Main Line would never come near here, I thought ruefully.

Heading up the well-worn wooden stairs, we scrutinized the second- and third-floor bedrooms and bathrooms: a sagging, rusted bedspread here, a thickly cobwebbed corner there. The rooms were empty, barren; as cold as the weather outside. Life had gone out of the place. It was depressing.

We said little to each other. We contented ourselves with random remarks. "There's a bathroom over here." "This window overlooks the roof of the shop next door." "Let's take a look at the third floor." I was no longer sure how to react. Here we had a whole hotel, but we also had sagging walls to plaster and paint, ceilings to repair, and plumbing to replace. A few faucets were left in place, but only a ghastly squealing noise came out when they were turned on. Each of the problems was easy enough to push aside, and my elation would return. The prospect of putting a roof over the heads of people we had to leave shivering on the cold streets night after night no longer seemed impossible. That thought excited me even as we looked to the tremendous work ahead.

Back on the first floor, while I was trying to get my bearings and visualize how to use the building, Father Domenic surveyed room to room with short, brisk steps. He looked like a building inspector checking the premises: opening doors, looking into closets, trying window locks, and tapping walls to test for structural soundness.

On his second trip to the kitchen area, my friend pulled open the pantry cabinet doors only to find much evidence of a mice encampment. Grimacing at the smell, he exclaimed, "What a burden this will be!" I had the impulse to take the key right back that second to Miss Dorothy at the Peace Mission Church.

My elation began to change to uncertainty as I followed him to the front entrance. When he turned right to the living area, I blindly followed him. He brushed a battered old couch with his hand and the dust swirled up in billowing puffs. He shrugged his shoulders and sat down. I sat next to him, waiting. He said nothing at first. He let his eyes inspect every corner of that room and a gentle smile crept to his lips.

Then he took my hand, bowed his blonde head, and began to pray in a firm quiet tone. "Lord, watch over this place. Give Trevor and his family what is needed to take in these poorest of the poor, these weakest of the weak, these forgotten people of the streets. Help him give what is needed to put a roof over their heads. Most of all, help him to give them the love they need so desperately. Help, O Lord. Help. We place our trust in you. Amen." "Amen," I echoed in a hushed whisper.

Anyone looking through those broken venetian blinds would have seen two men with their eyes closed sitting on a beaten-down couch in a drafty abandoned hotel, thirty-three rooms of emptiness. No one could have seen what was going on inside me. My priest friend's simple prayer had taken command of my spirits. I was caught up in a soaring emotion of faith, of love, of hope. It was a moment of celebration. My doubts disappeared.

Thank God Father Domenic did not choose that moment to launch into a discussion of plumbing, electricity, certificates of occupancy, heating costs, and all the other practical things he had learned in his own efforts to house the homeless in church and school basements and emergency shelters. Instead, from our first visit, we put our trust in the Lord. It was a moment that I can never forget. A deep sense of peaceful affirmation settled inside me. Words can't describe it. I knew then—without any hesitation—that this abandoned hotel would be revitalized as a haven of love and hope.

Father Rossi and I locked the front door, hugged each other goodbye, and parted. After he drove away, I sat and stared at the building. I tried to envision Sonny, June, and a multitude of others sitting outside on the steps. I couldn't yet, but I knew as the work inside and out progressed, I would. For me, Trevor's Place—A Home for the Homeless, was born at that moment on March 16, 1984, less than three months after our first trek downtown.

Even before we wrote a formal letter to accept the hotel, another phone call offered us free legal assistance. Trevor's initial simple gesture of concern had spiraled to a point where we no longer knew how to proceed. Deeds and grants, book and film inquiries left us reeling. A prominent Philadelphia law firm located in a high-rise in the very center of the city offered its services. We had often driven past it, when it was dark and unused, on our runs downtown. A member of the firm had seen the first TV news report and followed the papers' accounts; she had then described our efforts to the partners. A general discussion prompted them to offer the finest legal aid in Philadelphia, gratis. I found it confirming to know that the powerless poor who slept in the doorways of Philadelphia would benefit from the services of these power brokers. The haves and have-nots were building a new bridge.

Almost simultaneously, we discovered a group called Resources for Human Development, an organization designed to help fledgling groups provide social services in the Delaware Valley. They responded to our needs with office space, encouragement, advice, and help with our tax status as we began to take steps toward becoming a nonprofit organization.

Bob Fishman, the executive director, spent much time and effort helping me understand all that was involved; he also took care of the initial financial responsibilities. He came quickly to a deep understanding of what we were about. Bob, from experience, explained aptly the relationship between the spirit of the work and the realities we would face in opening up Trevor's Place. "Operating the house without a professional staff calls for a conscious leap of faith. This is not the way this kind of housing effort is normally begun, but we will stand behind it. There is need for this kind of risk taking. If we went to the city as a corporation and said we'd like to open a shelter, it would take us three to four weeks to find the right person to talk to."

Bob was right. Our efforts raised themselves up almost without conscious approval or plans. We had not followed the rules. We never considered that our family would become leaders in helping our city's 10,000 homeless. It all did seem a little crazy. It happened so fast.

The onslaught of attention and support, coupled with the ever-growing number of street people that looked to us for help and hope, began to define the work. We needed a name for the ministry that sprung up and for the documents we had to file. Susan Greenspon, the very first reporter to report on our efforts in the *Main Line Times* had coined the phrase, "Trevor's Campaign." It seemed appropriate. Thus Trevor's Campaign was officially born.

The papers and media had often referred to Trevor's Campaign in the previous months, simply from the need to have a name or label. When the term was used loosely, we never gave it a thought; but to accept that, in a span of weeks, a full-fledged legal organization that bore the same name was our responsibility—that was another matter. Suddenly, I became, along with Janet, the acting manager, renovation foreman (we learned the plumbing would cost us nearly $20,000 to repair), and fund-raiser for a run-down residential hotel. I was also publicist and chief executive officer of an organization boasting an ever-growing group of volunteer workers. The lack of time to adjust sent our lives into a tailspin. Each day I spent more time at work on the phone with volunteers to coordinate that night's run, or the next upcoming visit by a church or school group, than I did waiting on customers. When I arrived at home at 5:20 P.M., just as I had for years, what used to be a few bills and personal letters for me to deal with had turned into a bundle addressed to either Trevor or the Campaign that required a thick rubber band to keep it all together. The phone rang incessantly. A flock of reporters, ministers, college professors, social scientists, a book publisher, and several film producers—all requested personal time and attention. When added to the normal realities of a diverse and active six-member family, maintaining a stable sense of order or priority became impossible. I didn't even have time to think through my activities. I just woke up in the morning and plunged in.

I was almost completely absorbed in the Campaign. Meanwhile, Liza, my firstborn pride and joy, was learning to drive in between needing a ride to work at the ice creamery after dark and deciding whether to attend the high school dance or church party. She was ready to graduate from high school, cut the apron strings, and live a life of her own. College catalogs and applications covered the desktop in her room. When she was little, she was the focus of most of Daddy's attention. Now that she needed me in new and changing ways, I wasn't very available to her.

Young Jody, our eight-year-old, deserved the same kind of time that Liza had received at her age, but there wasn't as much of me to go around anymore.

After one too many responses of, "I'm sorry, Allen, I can't right now," my son quit asking me to try out his new computer program or discuss the latest sci-fi novel he'd read.

Then there were Janet and Trevor. Trevor still liked to go downtown better than anything else, although he didn't like all the interviews or people telling him how wonderful he was. Yet it was Janet's life that had really turned upside-down overnight. My willingness to let Trevor take one blanket and one pillow downtown had led to this. She didn't have much choice in the matter when suddenly pots and pans and people began filling up our lives. Both of us were living at full throttle. I couldn't carry on through all of the changes and projects without her support. But I knew her needs weren't being met. Time to nurture our personal relationship required strict planning and discipline to schedule and actually keep when a multitude of other demands horned in.

Janet was the straightforward partner in this enterprise. She confronted both me and the street people as to what motivated us into action. With her grounded wisdom, she often forced me to face reality when my heart was more in the clouds, dreaming about what might be ahead, than with the crisis way of life that demanded our attention on the streets. She was tired. "Not another casserole dish, please," was a weekly request. Stretched beyond previous limits, the whole family was feeling strained.

I knew that somewhere, somehow, something had to give. Balancing family, work, and the Campaign was virtually impossible without one facet of our lives suffering tremendously. The family wasn't an option to cut back on. I felt the decision was like drawing straws, and the lots were still even on my electronics business and helping the homeless. I didn't see how we could go on without either one, but I couldn't keep up like this for much longer.

Soon after the Poplar building received its christening as Trevor's Place, volunteers acting as painters, upholsterers, and housecleaners began working as furiously as funds for supplies and their schedules allowed. Restoration was happening, but we still had to leave men and women huddled against the bitter winds and hard asphalt each night. Occupation of the building was months away.

At home, during a late April rainstorm, the Ferrell household slept. Alone in my favorite room I read through a pile of unopened mail. On a piece of torn notebook paper, a nineteen-year-old inmate in an Idaho prison hoped that "this doesn't sound ridiculous, but I cried as I read about what you're doing." A little boy, just seven years old, wrote

Trevor from Chicago. A man preparing for the priesthood saw Trevor on TV and wrote to thank him for serving as "a beacon of hope in these times that seem so dark." An aerogram from India was tucked in the middle of the bundle. That night the letters spanned every age, ethnic, and socioeconomic group.

The next-to-the-last letter bore a Michigan postmark. A ten-dollar bill fluttered to the floor as I pulled the message out of the legal-sized envelope. "For doing what I don't," it read. "Keep it up." Those last three words echoed in my head. "Keep it up." How could I? How I wished to do more. I wanted to keep up my business and family life and still help Trevor with the Campaign. There was no doubt that caring for even a few street people and saving them from the bitter wind with the hope of helping them toward self-sufficiency was worth everything we'd given thus far. Nonetheless, I was worried about paying our family's bills and nourishing our relationship ties. A fanatical dedication to compassion on the streets would force my family into sacrifices I had no right to ask of them.

With my head swimming in questions and confusion, I left the letters stacked on the floor and trudged to bed.

Within the week, with a microphone forced under my chin, a reporter asked me, "Mr. Ferrell, would you make the same decisions again if given the chance to relive that evening when Trevor first asked to go downtown?" I answered with assurance that I'd do the same things. But later that day as I drove along the Expressway toward an appointment with a lawyer, a staunch supporter of our efforts, I let myself fantasize. What if I'd replied, "Trevor, take my word for it, street people breathe, sleep, and eat on the streets of our city." What if I'd left the matter closed and the issue unexplored? What would my life be like at this moment? Wondering, I parked the car, entered the law firm, and rode the express elevator to a floor near the top.

The elevator opened to chrome planters lush with well-cared-for greenery. After a word with the receptionist, I was quickly ushered into the office. A warm handshake and greeting later, I was seated beside the long oak desk.

Unclear as to the reason for the meeting, I wanted to cut short the formalities. "Well, Ed, what's up?" I asked. My friend motioned for me to wait a minute and asked his assistant to hold all calls for a few minutes.

"Frank, I'll get right to the point with you. I invited you here to discuss some of the things I've heard from friends in the suburbs and other associates downtown."

"What's wrong?" I worried. He leaned back in his chair and put his hands behind his head. "Well, I've heard unkind comments about why you're doing all of this. Some people have even said to me when they find out that we are friends, 'You know this Frank Ferrell? Is he on some kind of ego trip or what? It seems to me that he is exploiting Trevor to milk a good thing for publicity. What kind of money is he making off this?' "

My face must have mirrored the blow I felt inside. I felt my shoulders sag. My body reacted as if all the air had been pushed out of me. I sat limp and silent. I felt totally misunderstood.

"Now Frank, I absolutely repudiated the remarks because I know the whole story, and they're wrong. If they'd seen your struggle and integrity face to face through the months, they wouldn't say such things." My friend, no doubt, saw my pain and tried to assure me. I attempted a feeble smile, but no reply came to me.

Defensively, I made retorts in my head. "Doesn't everyone help others for the satisfaction they get? Are all of the other volunteers on an ego trip too, just because they commit themselves to this Campaign? Maybe the publicity we've received is the real problem." From time to time Janet, Trevor, and I talked about our longing for no fanfare and less fuss. Even Trevor said that. A reporter asked him during a follow-up interview, "Now that you have a home for the homeless, what would you wish for?" With the directness only a child can muster, he replied, "For things to be simple again." We often spoke nostalgically about when it was just our family in the car and a handful of street people. We gave to those we found in need from what we had. Relationships and caring for each other was the focus. Now it was so complicated.

My lawyer friend interrupted my thoughts. "You need to speak openly and candidly about your financial and personal situation. I know you have given almost everything yourself to keep the work going. I know the sacrifices you've made. Even though Janet hates the thought of your private matters being broadcast, you don't have anything to hide. Your lives are no longer private. Your actions aren't just your affair anymore. The continual coming and going at your house proves it. Your family, because you cared, has brought street people into the hearts of thousands of other people, and now the public feels a need to be able to know what makes you tick. It's the price you pay, Frank, in order to continue loving the homeless and inviting others to do the same."

I went home and shared the meeting with Janet. Hotly, she retorted, "Who are these people? It's none of their business." But then she balanced out, acknowledging, "It's human nature, I guess, to be skeptical and suspicious. From a distance people can ask cruel questions. They don't know us." I was discouraged.

I hadn't been to my shop for a couple of weeks. It was temporarily closed, and I was trying to decide what to do. The family was living on savings, but with Liza heading to college in a matter of months, Allen just two years behind, and Trevor and Jody in private schools, that wouldn't last forever. Should we take that risk and believe the Campaign was God's work for us and thus our needs would be met? Or was I really an egomaniac exploiting his own son to meet some dubious psychological need, as some wondered?

During that first summer, I wasn't sure. I knew my heart and the compassion that motivated me. I wanted the Campaign to bloom. But the possibility of heading toward a full, jeopardizing upheaval for my family scared me silly. Janet, too, found herself bouncing back and forth about whether the security of our family should be sacrificed for this crazy whim. Less than excited about the prospect of facing financial ruin, our relationship tensed. We knew we'd changed over the months but being willing to risk giving up all we had to help those with nothing was a new matter. Was it worth it? How would we feel in a year?

The routine forced us to continue, almost by rote, as the decision hung in precarious balance. I couldn't help wondering who the grumblers were that questioned our reasons for helping the street people. I didn't know what to say to whom. I leaned heavily on the inner circle of volunteers and friends for support.

During my confusion, a first-class letter, just like hundreds of others, passed in front of me. It was from a policeman assigned to patrol the red-light district of Seattle. From the first sentence, the depth of his concern penetrated to my pained soul.

"I can't escape those wretched, forgotten, and discarded souls that litter the doorways and line the alleys of our nation's cities. Society's throwaways . . . America the beautiful—her garbage . . . And beneath the grime and lingering stench, these insignificant strangers are often so grateful, in magnified proportion, to a seemingly simple act of kindness.

"No longer do I see refuse. I see my mother, my father, my sister, my brother—my neighbor."

He continued on to cite with authority the same Biblical passages that I considered confirmation of our calling to care for those in need. The words of Jesus took on new power. "Whatsoever you do unto the least of these, you do unto Me and whatever you do not do to the least of these you do not do to me" (Matthew 25:31–46). "Be ye a doer of the word and not a hearer only' (Luke 18:9–14). The tears began to flow as I read verse after verse. This man understood our struggle and deep conviction from thousands of miles away—someone we had never met. He seemed to understand what we faced even better than those who saw us regularly.

"Frank and Janet, you are probably feeling overwhelmed and that is why I am writing—to encourage you. Please don't surrender this Campaign. You have blessed me and so many others, not to mention all of those whose tears you've tasted. I believe the homeless are going to be one of the issues of this decade. God is placing people such as you all over this country as his signalmen to sound the alarm—to wake up those pockets of 'insulated' society. Your voices are beginning to stir the sleeping giant. Soon America's people will rise to the cause in a spirit of giving to rid this nation of her shame."

I couldn't believe how this man sensed my need and saw our purposes, and then I realized why he understood so clearly: He too saw and experienced the real smiles and fears of the forgotten hundreds of thousands of individual people with no place to go each night in his work. They were his friends as they were mine. The homeless weren't statistics, they were people. He went further, "It's amazing, that sometimes your closest friends can be your biggest dissenters. Don't listen to the critics, listen to Jesus. Nothing is impossible to God. He will not fail you. What he has started, he will finish. Just look at what he has done . . . with what he had . . . one little family who were willing."

I reread that letter often. I know that policeman was a messenger of encouragement from God for me when I had no clarity. The signpost in front of me bore no pointers. Just a month before we took the first three homeless men into Trevor's Place, Trevor and I visited St. Francis Residence in New York City. We were still struggling to get the hotel in shape. Every time we made progress on furnishing the house, the improvements that weren't bolted to the wall were stolen. An unoccupied building in this neighborhood was a temptation to those on the prowl. We needed to allow people to move in as soon as we could, even without the kitchen or other facilities all in order.

We visited the St. Francis Residence on the recommendation of the church group. One of the members had seen a report on the ministry house after hearing us talk about our dream of housing the homeless. We wanted to see for ourselves how some Franciscan priests had ended up as landlords for the most demanding of the homeless: those, like June, with emotional problems.

It was inspiring. The Franciscans have placed a loving roof over the heads of one hundred men and women ranging from age twenty-six to seventy-five. Many had long histories of hospitalization. Rent was paid insofar as each was able with public assistance and other benefits as they were allocated to the patients by the various government agencies. None was ever turned away for lack of ability to pay.

Their church, St. Francis of Assisi, became involved with the homeless, and their relationships became the catalyst for renovating a ninety-nine-room hotel in 1980. For us it had been the continual visits in the van. The van headed downtown every night and then left, but Trevor's Place would always be there, a continuous living statement of our commitment to help the homeless. And someday, just like St. Francis Residence, Trevor's Place could serve the people in three essential ways. First, it would provide a place of warmth and security and a community to belong to. After the initial healing process and adjustment to a more structured way of life, training of some sort would be encouraged and advocated for those who were able; then the third step—finding ways for the residents to support themselves—would relegate the streets to the past, not an option for the future.

After Trevor and I returned from our visit, I began to see

Donated by the Peace Mission, this building on Poplar Street now serves as Trevor's Place, Home for the Homeless.

photo by Ralph Davis

Frank Lodato and Mike Shrank, friends from neighboring New Jersey, ask Trevor what to expect as they wait to join the nightly volunteers on the food van outside of Trevor's Place.

The Ferrell family in t[...]
home. In back: Jody,
Allen, Liza, and Trevor[...]
front: Frank and Janet[...]

photo by Ralph Davis

Twelve-year-old Trevor in the fall of
1984.

photo by Dan Miller

The first residents of
Trevor's Place join Frank,
Janet, Trevor, and Buck,
the canine mascot, on the
steps.

photo by The White House

President Ronald Reagan salutes Trevor at the White House on April 25, 1985.

Trevor meets Ernest
Borgnine at Universal
Studios in October 19

Dennis Weaver presents Trevor with the John Roger International Integrity Award on
October 26, 1984, in Beverly Hills. Arianna Stassinopolous and Carl Weathers look on.

photo by Ralph Davis

Barbara Eden congratu-
lates Trevor at the reception preceding the John
Roger Award ceremony.

Bill Bright, president and founder
of Campus Crusade for Christ
with Trevor after the "Celebration
of Hope" benefit concert for
Here's Life Inner City at Carnegie
Hall on April 23, 1984.

John Roger and Trevor make a guest appearance on the Merv Griffin
show on October 24, 1984.

photo by Ralph Davis

Chico emotionally accepts the cake decorated in honor of his thirty-ninth birthday from Trevor on June 29, 1984.

Trevor exchanges a hug with a downtown comrade —a nightly sight during the food delivery runs.

Trevor listens to a woman settled on a manhole at 17th and Walnut streets.

Trevor listens after giving a friend a cup of coffee and homemade hamburger.

Intent on her story, Trevor studies the face of one of his friends who frequents the corner of 12th and Chestnut streets.

Trevor offers a bag of food to an unknown man in a Philadelphia alley.

that Trevor's Place had become a magnet for the givers and the receivers alike. Soon after, we moved in the first three residents.

There was still a staggering amount to do in order to qualify for a certificate of occupancy. "Lots of perspiration will go into this building before we feel any inspiration," as one volunteer described it. For many weeks, volunteer teams of ten to twenty spent Saturdays and Sundays—their days off from work—doing things no one could ever pay them to do: Scraping peeling paint off the walls; plastering holes in the ceilings; mopping, sweeping, washing, and cleaning years of built-up grime and decay. I couldn't begin to count the times I said a clumsy, silent prayer. "Lord, I'm turning this over to you. I have no idea how we're going to solve this."

No matter how hard I tried to solve the problems, I just never learned to predict where the answers would come from. When we had no means to either raise or find the money to straighten out the plumbing, a donor heard about us from a friend who had shown a videotape of Trevor's work to some neighbors. From that one viewing, we received $20,000—enough to finish the plumbing work.

Then there was the problem of the kitchen: It didn't work. This meant that the three men who lived in the house had to depend on the food we brought in every evening. For many weeks there was no solution. We made do. The men had to wait for their hot meal until the van made its rounds. The makeshift arrangement allowed the men to survive, but there wasn't any way we could increase the number of occupants in the building, feed them each day, and still have food left for all of those on the streets after we made the first delivery at Trevor's Place. I began to inquire into the cost of buying a new stove or a new oven. As the renovations that were already underway depleted our funds, it looked like we'd have to delay inviting more street people to live at Trevor's Place.

At this crucial moment, our next-door neighbor stopped by to tell us that he had a new gas oven to donate. All it needed was a platform to sit on. I knew how to do the installation, but who could build a platform? None of our volunteers seemed to be available or skilled. But we were to find help that very evening. I stopped at a sprawling ranch house to pick up a tuna-and-rice casserole for the downtown run, and our volunteer's husband, who is in the construction business, offered his services and those of two carpenters in his employ. Just when we needed it, help again was offered.

Just about this time, one of our volunteers brought a report on homelessness to read to us during a run downtown. This particular report by a Task Force of the American Psychiatric Association was prefaced by its chairman, Dr. H. Richard Lamb, with a statement that "the chronically mentally ill have been cast adrift under conditions that most persons think can no longer exist in this country." Then he added: "Sometimes their situation was the result of inhuman treatment, but more often it seemed to be simply neglect."

Later in the report* two researchers pointed out what is at stake, something that goes to the core of what is obvious night after night on the streets of Philadelphia (and all other cities): "Homelessness today is not fundamentally a social service or mental health problem. It is a state of deprivation defined by the absence of a primary element of civilized life—a home."

Maybe we shouldn't have been surprised, but we were certainly shocked to be reminded that more care is taken to avoid cruelty to animals, horrible as it is, than cruelty to helpless human beings. We confronted this cruel paradox in the early months when one of the first three residents, Bob, asked if he could have a dog.

H. Richard Lamb, M.D., ed., *The Homeless Mentally Ill: A Taskforce Report of the American Psychiatric Association* (Washington, D.C.: The American Psychiatric Association, 1984).

We thought it was a great idea for Bob personally and for the house itself. We could use a watchdog, since the place had already been burglarized three times. We drove to an animal shelter with Bob so he could pick out a dog. It was love at first sight for a young, frisky, and pathetically thin German shepherd. The dog jumped all over Bob, kissing and licking him. Big, gruff, stolid Bob melted.

"OK," we said, "we'll take this one."

It was not that easy. The manager of the shelter subjected Bob to intensive questioning: Where do you live? How long have you lived there? What is the physical condition of the building? When the questioning was over and Bob piled into the back of the station wagon with the tail-wagging German shepherd, Janet put my thoughts into words. "It's crazy that people take such care about where a dog is going to live, but no one cares what happens to people who are released from institutions or to people who have no place to stay."

After finding Bob's dog, I knew it didn't matter anymore if our friends or the people who heard about the Campaign from some other source understood or affirmed the way we were doing things. We were exposed to the lack of dignity accorded a huge part of the population. We had to do what we knew to do to give back what we could to those on the streets.

The barrage of support and occasional criticism continued daily. Now, there was a difference. The letters of affirmation and cheerful responses weren't what got me through the day. The street man who spit at me one night couldn't deter me any longer. I was doing the best I could, as were Janet and Trevor and the whole of our family and volunteers.

After much soul-searching, dialogue, and prayer, I developed a firm resolve. Amidst the varying opinions that surfaced constantly, I settled one issue. I wanted to be judged not by what I said but by what I did. Those who voiced concern that we didn't credit the Lord enough or witness to the street people forcefully enough were countered by those who understood our approach and opposed by the journalists who constantly tried to keep us low-key, or worse, off the subject of a personal, active faith. There were those who accused us of propagating street life by making it too easy to survive. "If a free meal is always available, why should they ever feel any desire to get with it and find a job?" Others applauded with their support and belief in reaching out to the homeless and perceived them to be the hurt people they really were, no matter what the exterior portrayed.

To those who wondered if we were caring for the spiritual needs of the street people, I responded that when we touch the poor, we cannot help but touch their spirits as well, inasmuch as the body is the temple of the spirit. When we feed the body, we prepare the soul. When we reach out to those needy men and women of the streets in the spirit of the Lord, we cannot help but preach loud and clear the message of Christ.

I no longer needed to defend the Campaign or my motives or Trevor's involvement. This was God's work, and the blessings bestowed upon us all confirmed it frequently. Each time a smile broke through on a formerly reticent or gruff face, we knew God was at work in us, building bridges. The sound of a "God bless you" resounding through littered alleyways when a woman was given a clean bedspread to wrap herself in against a windy, drizzling night put everything into perspective. At such times I deeply experienced being in touch with God. It was so right to experience a sense of harmony with the Lord of Creation through moments of sharing with another human being. Those sacramental seconds were not the stuff most days were made of. Life wasn't usually that clear; but each time the act of giving transcended the circumstances and brought deep joy, I knew we had to go on loving.

So it was that one bright sunny morning in early September, only nine months after we first went downtown, that I stood in the middle of my electronics store and looked at empty shelves, boxes filled with merchandise, a dust-covered cash register, and assorted debris accumulated after many years.

The notice in the window announced to my faithful customers: "Thank you for your patronage and loyalty for the past 19 years. I don't know where Trevor is going to lead us with all this and we may be back to open our door again."

The reality of leaving the business I sweated to build washed over me with a flood of mixed emotions. I needed to do something I rarely did. I prayed aloud. "Lord," I said, "I need a sign, some kind of clear sign. Am I making the right decision to close down my business?"

My voice sounded so strange in the emptiness of the store that I didn't say any more. But the thought kept running through my mind. I reminded the Lord of my situation. *A sign, Lord. A sign, please. Give me something to guide me. Look at me, Lord. Here I am, walking away from the business that has supported my family, that has enabled me to provide for their needs, even enabling me to send my children to private school. Now I'm about to turn my back on this business in order to devote my life to advocacy and aid for the street people. I need a sign, Lord.*

I picked up a large cardboard carton and walked out to the van parked in front of the store. The bright sunlight forced me to blink. While I tried to focus, a customer who I knew casually appeared seemingly out of nowhere. She walked steadily toward me. "Frank," she assured, "you've made the right decision. The Lord is behind you in this."

I was speechless. Chills shot through me. Peering over the box I held, I stammered something like "Thank you, Mrs. Morris. Nice of you to say that." I guess I reacted oddly, but I was too stunned to say anything else.

I packed the box and went back into the store, wanting to call Janet. I realized that I had already called the phone company to disconnect service, and I thought twice about calling from the pay phone outside. Janet would say that I'm overdoing it. Yes, the woman spoke the words I needed and wanted to hear. So what?

I put the thought out of mind, picked up another carton, and made another trip to the van.

Then it happened again. This time the assistant pastor of the Church of the Covenant in Bala Cynwyd came up to me. With his hand on my shoulder, he said, "Frank, we're all behind you in this."

I had been going in and out of the store for weeks after I temporarily closed it down, checking on the premises, clearing things out, passing dozens of people. Never once had anyone come up to me with a pat on the back or an encouraging comment. Yet on the one day that I prayed for an answer, these two people—one right after the other—came forward out of nowhere, affirming what I knew. There was no turning back, I had to go on.

Only a week later, the September 12 issue of *The New York Times* set forth the financial facts of the Campaign in a progress report about the occupancy of Trevor's Place. The reporter pointed out,

> Still, the Ferrells have paid a price for their work. They had been living on savings since Mr. Ferrell, finding himself overwhelmed by the demands of Trevor's Campaign, a few months ago closed a television repair business that had enabled him to maintain a house with a swimming pool and send his children to private schools. Trevor, who acknowledged "just average" grades, will have to repeat the sixth grade because of time lost from his homework. And Mrs. Ferrell concedes that she often feels tired as a result of "washing so many pots and pans."

The three of us, involved from the onset, paid a heavy price to open the doors of a dilapidated old hotel for what most of society called riff-raff. But for us, our dream to go back to the days of intimate time with a few street people who had so much to teach of gratitude, esssentials, and a survival way of life, was again possible. Trevor's Place replaced the blue Volkswagen van as a new haven for healing to happen. It was worth it.

6
Amazing Grace:
Trevor and Chico

As I stopped for a red light in center city, I glanced at the body slumped in the back of the van. The man had the forlorn and battered look of a middleweight fighter struggling to regain his senses after a dazing blow before the ten count was pronounced and he'd discover he lost the fight. Blood oozed from a cut over his left eye, his nose was swollen and darkened with bruises. There was pain in his eyes, a look of impending defeat.

He coughed feebly. Amidst his drunken murmurings I heard four garbled words, "I miss my father . . ."

I was irritated. That was Chico behind me. And this wasn't the first time we'd found him slumped over a steam grate, falling-down drunk after a recent disappearance from Trevor's place. We knew that if we hadn't seen him for a while, he'd most likely gone back to his old ways of drinking and sleeping on the streets. He acknowledged when sober that he was killing himself, and yet look at how I'd just found him!

My eyes focused on the green light ahead. I punched gas into the accelerator and drove on. Chico continued talking to himself. All of the personal details I knew about Chico he'd divulged in similar drunken states. His normal reserve dropped. I didn't feel like I knew or at least understood this Chico. The quiet, unspoken warmth of his black-brown eyes was the mode of communication I was more familiar with.

Weeks ago, over a paper plate of macaroni casserole and a

cup of steaming coffee, Chico had wordlessly spoken to Trevor with his eyes. Lying on a grate with a wine bottle poking out of his green army coat, Chico had only said "yeah" when asked if he were cold. He snuggled into the sleeping bag Trevor gave him. "Pretty warm," was his only response. Trevor somehow understood Chico's needs and his inner warmth, and thus Chico was ushered to the fore-front of our relationships with the street people.

Nearly every night thereafter, Chico approached the van. If Trevor wasn't able to come that night, he'd ask, "Where's my man? Where's Trevor?" There were other nights when Trevor would have to wake Chico up from his drunken sleep. As he blinked Trevor into focus, a happy greeting would rise to his face from somewhere deep inside. To watch the handsome Hispanic man and little boy embrace was to participate in a holy exchange.

Chico swears he'll never forget one particular night when Trevor strode up to him with an impish look in his eyes, his hands behind his back and a teasing tone in his voice. "Chico, I've got something for you." Chico tried to sneak a look at the hidden parcel, but Trevor turned each time, just in time, to keep the surprise he bore unseeable. Finally, when Chico gave up, Trevor presented him with a decorated birthday cake. That night Chico turned thirty-nine years old. Taken aback but visibly delighted, Chico whispered, "It has writing on it. It says my name." Yes, Chico, it was for no one else but you!

Only days later Trevor spotted Chico walking ahead of the van on Sansom Street. "Stop, Dad," he pleaded, "something's wrong with Chico's arm!"

Trevor scrambled out of the van and hollered Chico's name. Chico turned around at the sound of Trevor's voice. "There's my little buddy," he welcomed, one arm out-stretched to Trevor. The other coat sleeve dangled empty in the breeze.

My son's young face was furrowed in concern. "Chico, what happened to your other arm?" By this time Trevor had caught up with him and reached gingerly toward the empty armhole.

Chico quickly grabbed Trevor's chin and lifted the boy's gaze to meet his own. Laughing apologetically, he explained, "It's just part of panhandling. It's part of the scam, my little man."

Trevor relaxed but remained a little distant. He was seeing firsthand the con involved in the vocation of asking passersby for spare change. The amputee fraud was a ploy to get sympathy. Trevor didn't like it. Chico quickly pulled his arm out from the torn lining in his long army coat and put it in the proper sleeve. Soon the two friends were back to chatting as usual. But that incident reminded me of tonight. The drunk who could mislead people to get enough money to buy more booze was the man I hauled in the back of the van tonight. But he was also Chico, my lovable friend—a special part of our entire family. I was struggling with the reality that he was both the conniving drunk and Trevor's close, delightful friend. The life of a street man held some of the complexities of my own. How does one maintain a place in a particular society while doing what one feels he must do? Chico felt he had to drink, and he did what he knew would bring in the necessary money, even though it rankled in me as dishonest and manipulative.

I, on the other hand, was a middle-class male who'd developed a strange impulse to help street people. Those from what used to be my peer group couldn't understand why I'd made the seemingly crazy choice to give up my secure business and continue in this new way of life, any more than I understood why Chico panhandled to propagate his alcoholism. He was hooked on liquor, I was addicted to helping the homeless. We were a strange human pair that night as I drove Chico back to his new home, at Trevor's Place.

As I led him up the stairs to the room he proudly kept spotlessly clean, I realized he was still talking about his family. . . .

"My father, he died of a heart attack in his seat, in '76. He forgot to take his medication. He took a drink, went to sleep. He never woke up."

"What about your mother, Chico?", I asked.

"She's still alive. In Alabama."

"Have you talked to her lately?"

"Last year, I called her up to wish her happy Mother's Day. She sure was surprised to hear from me. That's the last time I talked to her."

"Do you think maybe you'd want to clean yourself up and go down to see her sometime?"

"I don't know. That's hard to say, Frank."

"But do you enjoy living out there on the streets? You know this winter is projected to be one of the coldest in years. You'll freeze."

"Well, I already put in three winters out there."

"I'd like to see you get yourself straightened out. You have a trade, don't you?"

"Landscape gardening."

"There's a lot of work that needs doing."

"What? Cutting grass?" he said, as he plopped down on his bed.

"No, not just cutting grass. Planting lawns, planning gardens, tending shrubbery and flowers. That sort of thing. You know what I mean."

But by then Chico was drifting off. I looked at the fully dressed man laying awkwardly sprawled across his quilted bed. Shoes still on, his eyelids fluttering a little in his light sleep. I turned off the lights and trudged down the steps.

I left Chico and drove back alone to the suburbs. I felt suspended between worlds—Chico's world of those who live in the shadows wrapped in an overcoat of anonymity, and the world of the Philadelphia Main Liners who own the grass and manicured lawns that Chico could tend if he'd stay sober.

By the time I pulled into my driveway I was emotionally and physically spent. I couldn't do any more for Chico tonight, but tomorrow was another day. I'd think about it then.

The house was still. As I headed toward the master bedroom, I stuck my head inside Trevor's door. He lay sleeping, his arms flung out wide across his bed. I knew he was no wonder child, but he'd been the one to reach out and prove to Chico that someone really cared for him. Something very rare exists between Trevor and Chico, you'd think they were brothers separated by a large age gap or long time friends instead of a Hispanic street alcoholic and a white suburban sixth-grader.

Seeing Trevor at rest rekindled my memory of him as a little boy. Sometimes now I felt I hardly knew this kid. Who was this compassionate son of mine? And what made him receptive to the Chicos of this world? Even when he was barely more than a toddler, he'd felt cut off from other kids. He pronounced his words awkwardly and the kids couldn't understand him, so they taunted him. When they didn't understand him, he would say, "Nayah mine" or "Fohget iya," which meant never mind, forget it. Once, even with all his problems in speaking, he told a strange story in front of his preschool class. The story, according to his teacher, was about a family that took a walk in the woods near their house. The family got lost and tried a shortcut, but was bewildered because no one recognized the landmarks even though they were in home territory.

I wondered now whether that was the story of the Ferrells, trying to help the street people and getting lost in the forest of human, emotional, psychological, economic, and governmental problems. We are wandering around looking for shortcuts and for some way to lead lost people like Chico out of the woods. And sometimes, even though we're not much more than a dozen miles from where we've lived our whole lives, everything is foreign and bewildering.

Over the last months I'd watched Trevor struggle to communicate his feelings about his new way of life. He managed to get his point across even without a polished set of phrases. People from David Hartman on "Good Morning America" to adult parishioners had commented on his poise time and again. The child sleeping before me never tried to make a good impression. He just tried so hard to tell people what he had seen on the streets and what he was trying to do.

I had to smile. I remembered when one interviewer had asked Trevor how he'd met Chico. Unthinkingly, he said, "Oh, in the normal way you meet somebody; he was laying on a steam grate . . ." Janet and I had burst into laughter. Trevor had come to think meeting friends on steam grates was typical. I was proud of Trevor and his simple reasons for loving Chico. I turned off the lights and walked on down the hall. It had been a long day.

The more time we spent with Chico, the more we learned about both his life and life on the streets. "Where were you before you ended on the steam grate, Chico?"

"I was in jail, Mr. Frank. And before that I was sleeping on a grate because my welfare payments were cut off. Without any money, a person got to sleep on the streets. If he got any good friends, they might let him stay there until he got back on welfare or go to jail. I go in for six months to get out of the cold. You steal something or cuss out a cop, then cuss out the judge and get six months. But that's not what I did when I went to jail. I was framed on a robbery charge and I served sixteen-and-a-half months for it.

"Before that, I was with my brother, the fireman. He got married to this New York Puerto Rican woman and she told my case worker that I did not live there, so they cut me off welfare. So back on the streets.

"I'm used to sleeping outside. When a person hitchhikes

from Philly all the way up to Maine twice and back, and then from Philly to Key West seven times, he gets used to sleeping anywhere. At nighttime you don't get rides. You gotta sleep outside. On the side of a highway, in somebody's cow pasture, or in somebody's apple field. You get used to it.

"It's hard to say how I got started on the grates. Well, in the winter, it's cold out there and there's heat on the grates; there ain't no other place to go. You lay down and go to sleep and hope to wake up the next morning."

Chico was swinging a broom furiously back and forth across the steps at Trevor's Place as he talked. Janet looked up at him and put her paintbrush down in the paint can. Matter-of-factly, she asked, "But Chico, why did you start drinking? Isn't sleeping outside bad enough?" The tall, smiling man lost his smile and shrugged without a word. Janet persisted, "Okay, but where'd you get the money to drink?"

"Panhandling, ma'am. Between two or three of us we'd collect enough for two, sometimes three gallons. One gallon of red wine costs $8.67. Money is easier to come by on Thursday, Friday, and Saturday. On those good days we'd always start with a fifth of Wild Irish Rose. That always gets the juices flowing."

"But Chico, aren't you afraid when you're drunk of what somebody could do to you? You can hardly stand up, let alone defend yourself!" Janet's voice crackled with intensity.

"When ya go to sleep, ya gotta know the neighborhood. Ya only sleep in your territory. Ya gotta know the cops. There's this one black cop in the 6th district who calls me 'cowboy.' One time me and Dirty Bob—a black dude—and his woman Mary was staying down there in a hooch by a laundrymat. The cop car would drive up and this guy would yell out, 'Hey, cowboy, come here.' I'd crawl out of my sleeping bag and go over to him. He'd pass me three cups of coffee with lids. He always remembered cream and lots of sugar. 'Give one to your buddies—and get back over here.' I'd hand over the coffees, stashing one for myself by my bag. Then, the cop would give me three take-out boxes with eggs, toast, potatoes, and jelly. There's good police who'll watch out for ya out there, as long as they know you ain't bothering anybody. Some lady used to come by and hand us clothes out of her car window."

"But the police are only there every once in a while, Chico," Janet prodded. "How else do you keep yourself safe?"

"Janet," Chico answered quietly, "you're never really safe. But we watch out for each other. You never sleep alone without somebody knowing where to find you. Sometimes you leave the buddy you're sleeping beside. You walk all around to your other friends on the grates. You shake 'em and ask, 'You okay, man?' They do the same for me. We make sure no jitterbug or junkie rolls us or beats us up over nothing. Sometimes, if a punk does steal your money or your bottle, we share. If you got a bottle you always say, 'Here, take yourself a swig.'"

Janet shook her head. "I can't comprehend what all goes on out there, or why you keep drinking. But Chico, you have a great heart. You're okay."

Chico just smiled shyly and kept sweeping.

Days later the telephone rang. It was Chico. "How'd I get here, Mister Frank?" his sober voice asked. "I'm in a hospital in Jersey. How'd I get here? I can't remember." Chico sounded panicked.

"I was more than drunk last night, Mr. Frank, I was oxy-fied. I must've had a blackout. I woke up this morning in a de-tox unit. I looked out the window and all the cars had Jersey tags. How'd I get across the bridge from Philly? I don't remember anything."

Linda, a volunteer from the Main Line, was responsible for taking Chico to Memorial General. She'd taken him from hospital to hospital. "No room." "All full." "No beds." "Does he have insurance?" These were the answers she kept getting. But if she had to, she'd just take him home with her to her sprawling house. Linda wouldn't give up, and still she found resistance to accepting even one more disheveled drunk. Finally, she got him admitted in New Jersey—not because someone cared, but because her husband was a prominent physician.

"Frank, I've never been in Jersey before," Chico admitted. "It'll be okay, Chico. Just stay there and get sober. It's okay."

After that, Chico was sober for a time. He looked good, seemed content, and helped out with cleaning at Trevor's Place. Then Chico left without a trace.

Each night on our rounds we'd ask those in his usual neighborhood, "Where's Chico, have you seen Chico?" No response. We all were beginning to worry. On Thursday the phone rang. "Hello, Frank Ferrell?"

"Yes, this is he," I replied. "This is Henry Vanderhoff. My wife and I would like to accompany you some night this week as you help the street people." "How about tomorrow, Mr. Vanderhoff?" "Fine, Mr. Ferrell." I instructed, "We'll meet at 6:30 P.M. at our house in Gladwyne." "What can we bring?" Mr. Vanderhoff wondered. Immediately, I said, "How about franks and beans?" "Fine, we'll be there at 6:30 P.M. Goodbye." "Goodbye, Mr. Vanderhoff."

I returned the receiver to its cradle and dropped into the chair by the phone table. Henry Vanderhoff was perhaps the most sought after financier in Philadelphia. I'd heard his house had five security gates and gold-plated fixtures in each bathroom. He and his wife were regulars in the *Philadelphia Inquirer* social columns. And I'd just asked Henry Vanderhoff to make franks and beans.

"Trevor, you've done it to me again," I laughed softly.

Friday came, and at 6:25 P.M. a well-waxed Cadillac Seville wheeled around the cul-de-sac and parked across from the house. A gray-haired gentleman helped a gentle looking, carefully coiffed woman out of the passenger side of the car. The man carried a large covered casserole. Henry and Marilyn Vanderhoff had arrived.

I extended my nervous greetings and Janet joined me. She'd changed clothes after working at Trevor's Place all day. I saw her glance at the van—food stains were visible through the open door even from the end of the driveway. She was thinking, "The Vanderhoffs are going in there with us."

Then Trevor rode up on his motorbike. "These are the Vanderhoffs, Trevor." "Hi," he said, and looked back at me. "I hope we find Chico tonight." That's all. No fanfare. He didn't care if the Vanderhoffs were wealthy, important people in the city; he was worried about Chico. He parked his motorbike in the garage and hopped in the van.

Soon we were on our way. Henry and Marilyn didn't wait to be shown what to do. At the first stop they grabbed ladles and began dishing up the food. There were those franks and beans. One old woman spilled her juice on Marilyn's sleeve, but she barely noticed. I was impressed. I guess I'd expected them to be ill at ease or different from our other volunteers. They weren't. They were wonderful.

Near the end of the route we passed a one-way street. "I think that's Chico down there," Trevor pointed excitedly. "I think that's him!"

We had to circle the block to get onto the one-way street. The man wasn't Chico, but as we drove two more blocks up the one-way street, we saw him, slumped against some steps in a doorway at 10th and Sansom. The detour had led us to him. He was so drunk he couldn't stand, and his eye was bloody again. The perpetual bottle was visible in his coat pocket.

"C'mon, Chico," Trevor commanded, "we're going to detox." He grabbed his hand to help him up. Chico pulled his hand away. "No, tomorrow, little buddy. Don't want to go tonight."

"You have to go tonight. Now, Chico." Trevor insisted. Chico relented. Janet grabbed his left arm and Trevor his right. Chico was too heavy. They all collapsed on the steps.

Henry stepped out of the van. He half faced Chico and swung the inebriated man's limp arm around his shoulders and braced his feet against the cement steps. Trevor and Janet supported Chico's other arm. Awkwardly and wobbling, they helped him to his feet and steered him toward the van.

The street lights barely illuminated the scene. In the dimness of a damp, humid evening in the heart of center city, a boy, his mother, and the patriarch of a leading Philadelphia family supported a drunken man.

"Watch your feet! Watch your feet!" Chico started to insist loudly. Henry and Janet looked at each other quizzically. What was he talking about?

"Watch your feet!" Suddenly Chico straightened up by his own accord. He grabbed his bottle and hurled it onto the sidewalk. Shattered glass flew in every direction.

Trevor was the first to understand. "That's Chico Power!" The few pedestrians nearby noticed what had happened and actually applauded.

"I'm doin' this for Trevor. I'm doin' this for Trevor," Chico declared.

We managed to get Chico into the van for the trip to the de-tox center. We said a prayer all together and then sang in unison "Amazing Grace." We had to depend on Chico, who was the only one who knew all the words. The song reverberated in the van as we sang our hearts out. It was Chico's epiphany. It was our shout for Chico's salvation.

At the medical center, we were directed from the emergency unit to the de-tox center, where a big, burly security guard confronted us. He called the admissions nurse. Her reaction at the sight of yet another drunk was, "We don't have any beds!" She didn't want to have any part of Chico and his entourage.

Then the guard intervened. With another glance at Trevor, he whispered, "Isn't that the kid who was on television?" He turned toward the nurse, "Hey, Mayor Goode gave him an award. That's the kid who's working with the street people." The admissions nurse was still surly, "Whatcha talking about?" She continued shuffling papers, trying to make us disappear. At that point, a white-robed orderly from the emergency unit appeared to say, "Trevor, when you're finished here come back to the hospital, because they're taking up a collection."

Then total silence.

We watched and waited.

The nurse quit working with her papers and walked out of the reception room for a moment. She came back to announce gruffly, "Well we've got a bed. Someone left. But you have to go over and get that eye fixed first."

Back in the emergency room as we led Chico to the doctor, Marilyn spotted a black woman writhing on a hospital bed. Pain was etched in the woman's furrowed brow. Marilyn spotted a doctor and asked, "May I try to soothe her?" The startled doctor said, "Sure." It was then that I noticed that the atmosphere had changed from indifference to friendliness toward our group.

Marilyn talked to the woman and learned that she lived with and took care of an eighty-year-old man. I looked at Chico sitting quietly as the intern sutured his eye. When I turned back to Marilyn I heard her ask the woman, who was in her thirties, if she ever listened to music. The woman said no, but that she watched television. When Marilyn responded, "Oh mercy, that's depressing," the woman laughed.

"Have you seen the little boy who takes food to the people on the streets on TV?" Marilyn continued. The woman nodded. "My sister's a street person." Marilyn offered to introduce Trevor. The woman perked up. Her writhing stopped immediately. Marilyn called Trevor, who was just on the other side of the hospital curtain that separated the beds.

With effort, the woman sat up in the bed to greet Trevor. She started to cry as she gave Trevor the benediction of the needy: "Oh, God bless you. You've been so wonderful. And you're so young."

An embarassed Trevor shook her hand, thanked her, and sidled away.

Alone with Marilyn again, the woman poured out her story. A stepfather who beat her as a child and padlocked her in a closet . . . her own resolve never to be like that as a parent . . . her drinking and then violent behavior against her own children . . . when she was drinking, she would sometimes pick up her own children and throw them . . . she lost custody of the children . . . she was desolate without them . . . she tried to stop drinking, but couldn't . . . without her children, she didn't feel there was anything to live for. . . .

Marilyn listened and spoke soothingly to the woman. "Well, you know God has a plan for Trevor's life. It started out to be a very small plan and it's grown. I'm sure God has a plan for your life, too. You just have to find out what it is and let him talk to you about it."

The tension was visibly draining from the woman. They prayed together and Marilyn left the woman at peace.

After making sure that Chico was taken care of, we got ready to leave. But before we made it out the door, a nurse stopped us. In the time since we had arrived at the hospital, doctors, nurses, and attendants had taken up that collection to help Trevor's campaign. She handed me a sealed envelope.

We drove home feeling depleted of energy, but full of thanksgiving. Something wonderful had just happened. It resounded in our depths, but we didn't talk about it. Everyone seemed to be lost in private thoughts. Each one had to examine the tired peace privately. Then I thought about Chico sleeping in a starched, sterile bed. I wondered whether we could ever really get Chico back on his feet. I prayed a silent prayer of hope.

7

"You Do Anything You're Asked to Do"

One hot, humid June morning, a pleasant-looking woman nearing seventy arrived in our driveway. Her gleaming white hair was covered by an azure scarf that brought out her pale blue eyes.

"Hello," she said when Janet greeted her at the front door. "I'm here to clean out Trevor's van. The volunteer coordinator sent me. It's wonderful to finally meet you."

Janet was taken aback. She ushered the visitor into the house and quickly came and found me. There was no more thankless, disagreeable, and dirty job to do in connection with Trevor's Campaign.

Months of spilled food, coffee stains, and sticky juice covered by the perpetual city dirt and grime had left the van in a disgusting condition. In hot weather, it had to be aired out every day to get rid of the rancid smell before we made our evening trips. And here on our doorstep was this polite stranger, neatly turned out in polka-dot blouse, tan skirt, and sandals.

While I talked to the volunteer, Janet phoned one of our coordinators. She asked her, "How could you ask anyone to do such a thing? How can you ask someone to clean that filthy, dirty van? What am I supposed to do? Stand around and watch her?"

The coordinator explained that the volunteers had offered to do anything at all, and the van had been on the top of the list. Janet hung up and rejoined us in the living room.

The situation became even more awkward. Janet and I had an appointment downtown, so we had to hurriedly excuse ourselves to finish dressing. As we backed out of the driveway, the woman was standing in dirty water mopping the floor of the van and washing down its interior walls. Janet was mortified. She was freshly groomed and looking her best. "I feel like a Main Line Lady Bountiful while that woman, who is my mother's age, is cleaning the van. And to top it all off, we drive off and leave her under the supervision of eight-year-old Jody. This is absurd."

That was the first time we saw Marge Gobay, a volunteer who sums up her philosophy of volunteering this way: "You do anything you're asked to do."

Janet and I never fully realized that people like Marge exist, ready to immerse themselves in a project and to do whatever needs to be done, whenever or wherever. These are not fair-weather volunteers, around from time to time to seek applause or a quick self-esteem boost. They could not be hired for money. They obviously work for the love of other people.

Marge is far from the only such volunteer who has emerged to help Trevor's Campaign. Neurosurgeon, salesman, student, housewife, graphic designer, bank teller, nurse, para-legal, contractor, lawyer, economist—volunteers have come from all directions. We never know when someone will appear. They usually phone after hearing about Trevor's Campaign from a friend, a newspaper article, a radio or TV program. Each time we answer their calls, we know we are in touch with another person who cares. As varied as they are individually, they always make it clear in one way or another that they feel like their "brother's or sister's keeper." They feel like an integral part of the human community.

Marge is a retired widow who worked for the U.S. Census Bureau. Her interest in street people was piqued during the two years before her retirement. Because she started work at

7:30 in the morning, she passed street people still sleeping in doorways as she walked from the bus terminal to the Federal buildings. At lunchtime, during warm weather, she ate her lunch in the park at Independence Square and noticed street people again.

An attractive blonde bag lady in her forties caught Marge's particular attention. The woman lived in public, going to the public toilet to change her clothes from her overflowing plastic shopping bags.

Every morning she would approach the public water fountain, remove a few layers, and quietly wash her face and body under her remaining clothes. She carried a small container of shampoo and would follow her bath with a thorough hair washing, filling up an empty glass jar she also toted daily to rinse the suds from her hair. Again and again she'd fill the jar and pour it over her head. What most people would do only in total privacy, this woman did in front of strangers, oblivious to her self-exposure. In the winter the woman would disappear and Marge would worry about what happened to her. Then she'd reappear in the spring. Marge wondered, "How do these people survive? What are they all about?" But she did not approach the woman, who was continually babbling to herself, seated on the same corner every day. She switched to screaming obscenities and nonsense words at times. The woman seemed unapproachable. But Marge's heart went silently out to her.

As soon as Marge retired at the end of 1983, she volunteered to work at Mercy Hospice for the homeless—coincidentally, she started on the same day that we made our first trip downtown looking for street people. In her own uncomplicated way, Marge was hoping that the bag lady from the park would come to the hospice for lunch and she could find out about her. It didn't happen, but Marge sorted clothing, cleaned rooms, served food, and washed dishes—whatever was needed.

The hospice experience had brought Marge into close

contact with street people for the first time. She admits that she was afraid at first, particularly of the men. But that soon changed. "I'm very much at ease now with the street people. I can easily do things for them. I love them. They're special people."

Soon after her initial experiences with the hospice, she heard Trevor and me interviewed on the radio. Marge called us to offer her services. Janet immediately sensed the caring quality in her voice. Not only did Marge express her readiness to volunteer, but she proceeded to describe what she had been doing at the hospice as if she were applying for a job. Janet assured her that she was what we needed, took down the information and asked our coordinator of volunteers to contact Marge.

From that phone call forward, Marge has amazed me. Her outlook on life is incurably positive, despite difficulties in her personal life that rival anything experienced by some of the street people. She started by volunteering every Tuesday and now, as she puts it, "I'm on call." Whenever any work is needed, the word is, "Let's ask Marge."

She cooks, she cleans, she works around Trevor's Place to make it look homey by adding a collectable figurine here, a pottery vase here. When she started to volunteer during the summer, her own apartment was being painted; but the job was not completed for months. She had a disagreement with the painter and, because she became so involved in fixing up the Poplar Street residence, never got around to getting the painting finished. Her own apartment still had no drapes when she made them for Trevor's Place. She spent much more time and energy fixing up a place for the homeless than in fixing up her own home. She laughs at that, saying she's always had a roof over her head and they haven't. "It's only justice at work!"

Marge has come to symbolize for me the person who is an initiator. She's a volunteer who goes directly from seeing a need to doing something about it. There's no intermediate stage. She doesn't have a great deal to say, nor is there any dramatic flourish. As a fellow volunteer and friend commented, "Marge is a doer, a spontaneous person. She doesn't want to be complicated. She's here and she's going to do what she can and let it go at that."

Peeling potatoes, mopping floors, cooking a casserole, waxing floors—there's no spine-tingling excitement involved in what volunteers like Marge are ready to do. They enjoy helping others. And they're not temperamental about doing routine things. Helping others never seems to be a chore. Experiencing such people firsthand was a revelation for me. Marge says giving isn't work, it's the highest form of fun.

Christine, another volunteer, aptly summarizes Marge's giving nature. "She's a woman who has a totally natural sense for people. She enjoys them tremendously. More than that, she loves people. She's a therapist without even realizing it. All she has to do is walk into the situation. People sense immediately that she really does care. She's a giver. She herself has a terrific outlook on life. She really enjoys it. She has the courage to simply be who she is, and that's therapeutic to anyone. Being with Marge is really an uplifting trip."

Christine herself is a mainstay, a pillar of active support. Like Marge, she cares deeply; yet it is Christine who reflects often on the total picture. Christine joined Trevor's Campaign "out of gratitude for the life that I had had." She had worked as a secretary before her marriage and then spent thirty-three years of her life as a suburban wife and mother before returning to work as an executive secretary. Back at work, she "felt the compulsion not to work for money: Anybody who has been as privileged as I had been—being taken care first by my father, then my husband—should be doing something with her life to care for others who hadn't been that fortunate.

"I don't see giving a part of my life to Trevor's Campaign

as anything virtuous at all; it's very logical. I've been given much and have much to give in return."

For her part, Christine has helped me to see the wider significance of Trevor's Campaign as she herself participates by serving food on the van and by assuming responsiblity for the enormous volume of correspondence that has been generated. She also prepares our newsletter.

Christine is the one who responds to the letters from a seventy-year-old woman and her seventy-four-year-old husband, who write to "share what we can" by means of a five-dollar check.

She's the one who says thank you to a woman who describes herself as "old and on Social Security. I wish I could send lots of money to help the street people." She's the one who discovers the beauty of the two crumpled dollar bills given by someone who barely survives herself.

For Trevor, and for Janet and me, Christine has become our pen and paper. She's able to express what we can feel deeply, but find difficult to articulate. She's the link between us, what happens day to day, and all of the hundreds of people that are a part of Trevor's Campaign. She keeps everyone up to date and thanked through the newsletters and personal letters.

As a central figure in Trevor's Campaign, Christine has spoken in person or by letter to perhaps thousands of people. Not all are supportive. She's faced the same criticism that we all have heard. "What you're doing is only providing help for one day. It doesn't change the situation."

Christine was the first to echo Mother Teresa's response to those who criticized her for "giving them fish instead of teaching them how to fish." She answered that the people she helps cannot stand; and if they cannot stand, they cannot hold a fishing rod. When they are strong enough to stand, then they can go to those who will teach them how to fish.

"That's pretty much how I see the street people," Christine emphatically adds. "They are people who have been broken in one way or another. Not all of them, but a large percentage of them have simply been too fragile to stand up to life's blows. None of us can judge them, because none of us knows their—or our own—breaking points.

"As for Trevor's Campaign, it shows that what one person can do is fantastic. Not only that—when everyone is saying that it can't be done, people are doing it. We have a challenge to be human and to work together . . . Mother Teresa made a wonderful comment. She said the poor don't need us half as much as we need them. Unless we have people to give to and help, we become very self-centered. The poor give us the opportunity to go beyond our selfish instincts and desires."

Christine is a woman of strong faith and deep conviction. She understands the direct connection between loving God and loving other human beings. She envisions faith as a two-way street. Loving God leads to giving to other people, and loving people helps us to find God. The two are inseparable.

Then there's Morris. When Morris adds his voice to the chorus of volunteers, I sometimes feel as though I'm hearing and seeing the Scriptures walking and talking alongside of me in very ordinary day-to-day experiences. Morris's words are few, his actions many. Each evening he pulls up to the house after making only he knows how many stops, his white Chevrolet brimming with casserole dishes and steaming pots and pans full of food. Thermoses of coffee line the floor. A jug of red punch or juice accompanies him in the passenger seat.

By day Morris works as a therapist for Horizon House, a drug rehabilitation center in the area. Raised in an established Philadelphia family and trained as an Episcopal priest, he grew up surrounded by upper-class affluence. Why someone from his background spends his life, nearly every minute of it, with those who have nothing, is something I'll probably never know. Morris talks about himself so rarely. But I know for a fact that the bottom line for Morris is love.

One Saturday afternoon in the summer the day was warm, almost balmy. Morris was in a rare mood, willing to talk about Trevor's Campaign. His long, lanky body was turned slightly sideways so that the easy chair could accommodate his height. His quiet voice formed slow, articulate phrases, and his hands were coaxed into action when emphasis was needed. His untamed white hair seemed almost transparent in the late afternoon sun.

When asked why he first got involved, Morris responded, "I think that to feed those who are hungry is very biblical. Clothe the naked, comfort the suffering, give warmth and shelter—these are among the most important and meaningful human tasks. Yet many adults are lethargic about this. It took the start by Trevor to get the adults involved. Now we probably have several hundred adults who consider themselves a part of Trevor's Campaign when you consider food, clothing, shelter, donations, all the different ways people help. I really believe that people act out of their deep conscience. I don't think guilt is the motive. Rather it is choosing to do what you see needs to be done."

Morris started by going downtown with us to deliver food and to distribute clothing, blankets, and pillows for two to three nights a week at the very onset of the campaign. Then he took over as driver for two or three nights a week. By the end of February—less than two months after we ourselves had started going downtown—Morris had taken over the seven-day-a-week task of making sure we had a supply of food to take to the street people. His help is unflagging.

That reflective day gave me a chance to find out something I'd been wondering about. "How do you keep going, Morris? Sometimes I feel as if I'm trying to dig out the Grand Canyon with my fingernails." Morris smiled knowingly. He knew better than most the burnout and fatigue we all struggled with. He paused to think, then answered, "I keep going just by momentum. Just by programming myself. I'm kind of a working machine, you know. Work doesn't bother me. It becomes routine. The more regular a task becomes, the more it becomes second nature.

"I guess, too, I have to admit the spirit of what's happening—the positive, loving atmosphere of everyone involved in this campaign helps a lot. People constantly show that they love and care about each other. Groups I've been associated with in the past tended to be political or academic, and they weren't as compassionate as I hoped they might be. But this group is very much for each other. The job can't be done by one or two individuals. It has to be a large corporate entity working together. I really see this happening. Each house I stop at, and each dish in my car, represents many hands who act out of concern for someone they don't even know.

"And then there are the street people themselves. They've given enough to keep me coming back night after night. Why would a person who's suffered most of his life want to be kind to somebody who's had lawns and trees and suburban ease—an easy life without the same pains and challenges? Why would they be kind to us? Yet we find ourselves extremely well accepted. We can then grow spiritually.

"People who are out here living comfortable lives are in danger of stagnating spiritually—of becoming wealthy, of becoming jaded, of becoming in need all the time of more entertainment, more trips, more shows, more money, more clothing. We are all in danger of that out here. By helping the street people, I can feel that my life is really worth something. Even though you live out here and live with the guilt of plenty, you still feel that your life is worth something when you can give something vitally needed to an individual who is hungry, cold, thirsty, lonely.

"I feel I'm lucky to oversee the network of people who

cook for the campaign. I continually experience and hear of the rewards giving bestows on the giver. There have been so many 'miracles.' I can still see Mrs. Godwin's face when she told me how much more alive she felt now that she was cooking for the campaign. She suffered from what she and her therapist both diagnosed as 'severe depression.' She read book after book, joined encounter groups and social clubs. Nothing helped. Then she heard about the campaign and began cooking and occasionally going out in the van. She claims the gratitude she received in return for helping made her begin to feel good about herself.

"I'm amazed at how a person can volunteer to cook once, and before I know it a spouse calls to offer to drive the van some night. I hear the children in the family proudly admit they peeled the potatoes or washed the vegetables when I ring the doorbell. In-laws, parents, and relatives are soon recruited. That's how over six hundred people have lent support to keep the giving spirit going. Now many call me before I get back to them asking, 'When can we cook next?' "

Morris went on to explain that, to his amazement, he noticed a trend whenever he telephoned a volunteer to help. He related a typical conversation. He'd ask, "Jane, can you make a hot dish for tonight?" And the answer would be, "Why thank you, Morris, for asking me. I'd be glad to."

"As I understand it," Morris summarized, "the volunteers are saying, 'Thank you for letting me see how simple giving can directly affect people's lives. Thank you for showing me a way to give that enables me to feel good about myself.' They thank me for allowing them to work. And these are all busy, busy people."

After Morris left that particular afternoon, I asked myself, "Where have I been all of these years? Why hadn't I appreciated so fully how important each person can be before?"

People like Marge, Christine, and Morris had always been a part of my life, no doubt, but it took Trevor's Campaign to help me recognize their worth. I knew at that moment that if the campaign were to end the next day, my family had been enriched beyond human measure by the volunteers. We were surrounded by a circle of concern and love. I'd learned from watching them just what giving means. They were the God-sent psychological support that kept us going.

I leaned back on the sofa, my hands behind my head, and envisioned Morris as I'd seen him many times, standing behind many a lectern speaking to church congregations about Trevor's Campaign. He constantly reiterated one main, encompassing theme.

I heard his serious, gentle voice in my head:

"This child, named Trevor, has led the way. We can all make our lives worthwhile by being willing to see other's needs and then doing something about it. We can give of ourselves physically by cooking, cleaning or driving. We can join our spirits in prayer for the continued strength and guidance. We can give money. Whatever we give of ourselves, we can be assured it helps to justify and add meaning to our lives here."

He had said all that needed to be said.

8

What It Takes to Love

I sat nervously in the high-backed, red velvet chair, staring out at the sea of well-dressed parishioners. I was waiting to hear my name called, the signal that I'd have to go through with this. I tried to convince myself that I should be used to speaking to large crowds by now, after all these months. I trained my eyes on the activities on the platform; maybe that would distract me.

The dark-suited minister stood, strode confidently to the teak-wood pulpit, and began to read: "From the words of the prophet Isaiah, chapter eleven, verse six: 'The wolf will live with the lamb, the leopard will lie down with the goat, the calf and the lion and the yearling together; and a little child will lead them.' "

There was the phrase again. Cornelius was the first one to connect that phrase to Trevor during the first winter. Bundled up, standing on a corner as the snow fell all around him, a Philadelphia TV news reporter asked the young man what he thought of my son. "I love that kid. When I first saw the van, I didn't like it. I figured they had an angle, just like everybody else. But then when Trevor, the kid, got out, I thought, 'Hey, that's just like the Scriptures said. They always said "a little child shall lead them." ' Then I knew it was okay."

Mother Divine used the same expression when she gave us the Poplar Street house. And Morris consistently reminded us of Trevor's leading.

As the minister concluded his introduction, I wished Trevor were with me. This was the only time he couldn't accompany me. Usually I counted on him to fill in what I left out. We never used scripts but depended on each other. I relied on the fact that something special happens when Trevor talks to people. Unassuming and simple, he attracts people with his quietness, his honesty. But today I was alone with my tan-colored volunteer sign-up sheets in front of a large congregation. This part of the Campaign was the hardest for me.

After the service when I was finally free from the well-wishers who encircled me, I joined a group gathered around our faithful volunteer Christine, who accompanied me. I heard one older woman say, "Don't you think it takes a special person or gift to work with those kind of people? They're unstable and obviously have so many problems."

Christine smiled, recalling her initial response to venturing downtown. "If I hadn't gone down there, I never could have believed that people just come out of the woodwork when the van appears." She continued, explaining that she was struck with the fact that the street people became individuals for the first time, instead of a part of a weird, frightening group. Some she felt close to and able to talk to, others she didn't. "It was just like any other new situation, meeting a bunch of people. You begin to see, in time, that you're building trust as you get to know each other."

"Unless you do it," she added, "you cannot imagine those eyes. Those eyes. I always see those people's eyes."

Christine contrasted the experience of going downtown intending to help someone, to what happened when she spontaneously tried to approach a woman while shopping downtown one afternoon. The woman, in her thirties, was wrapped in an old Indian blanket and looked as though she could hardly stay on her feet. She staggered back and forth across the sidewalk. Her eyes rolled wildly from side to side. She looked ready to pass out. Hesitant, uncertain about talking to the woman, Christine walked around the block to muster her courage. When she decided to approach and

headed toward her, she was driven back by a scathing re-
buff. "You just leave me be!" There was venom and violence
in the woman's voice.

Christine continued, "When I first went in the van to go
downtown, I sat next to Trevor. I told him about that woman
after a solitary street person, a man in ragged, torn jeans,
rejected his offer for food after the van had stopped just for
him. I'll never forget what Trevor said to me. 'You see, it's
like this,' he explained. 'It's just like a kitten, a little kitten
that feels strange. You put down a little bowl of milk and
first of all, the kitten won't come. Or if you get near it, it'll
shoot out its claws. You just do it again and again, and bit by
bit the kitten learns that it can trust you and then everything
is okay.' "

I stood listening to Christine talk about Trevor, and before
I realized what I'd done, I chimed right in. "That's what
happened with Greedy, a black man we saw each night
wearing a blue stocking cap. He rejected Trevor's plates of
food for the first few tries. At first he yelled obscenities and
told us, 'Get your food out of here.' Each night Trevor kept
approaching him, and soon we had to give him his nickname, Greedy, because once he'd said okay, he kept asking
for more and more food; 'More cream, more sugar, more
spaghetti.' Gradually, Greedy came to realize we cared
about him."

"When Janet took our son Allen away for a vacation,
Trevor greeted them at the airport with good news. 'Guess
what? Greedy is now friendly and nice.' When Janet asked
how it happened, Trevor said, 'I just kept trying. I was extra
nice, I'd give him extra food.' "

"Greedy was a challenge to Trevor, and he won him over
by sensing the man's needs. As Trevor explained, 'I was
thinking that he wanted more than anyone else because he
thought he was hungrier and more important than everyone
else.' Trevor's special attention won his trust."

After we left the church and drove toward Gladwyne in

Christine's car, we talked more about Trevor and why he was able to love some of the street people who resisted the most. I remembered reading about Project Help in New York City. They usually make fifteen to twenty contacts before a street person will accept help. Right from the start, the reason for Trevor's immediate acceptance on the streets has been obvious. He is a child. Adults, even our volunteers, are more apt to analyze or judge someone we meet. Children often can accept others more readily. Adults represent power and authority; children are dependent and vulnerable. Children are more likely to take things at face value and go from there. The young are more trusting; adults have to ask why before understanding.

Trevor brings a child's perspective into our downtown trips, and his worldview shapes the approach of adults who join us on our rounds. They follow Trevor's lead. That subtle adventure of opening up to a new experience and type of person allows the adults to actually meet street people as equals. "I think that the most important moment for new volunteers is when they give up any feelings of being givers and become participants instead in a learning, stretching experience. When they see the process of giving and receiving as a reciprocal one, they understand what the Campaign is all about."

Christine made another observation. "Trevor's approach is certainly contagious and we have all adopted it, particularly in the way we make contact without demanding case histories. That's the reason we don't have long biographies of the street people we know. That's why we can't deliver a play-by-play of how they ended up on the streets. I'm convinced that if we had an inquisitorial style, it would turn them off and the word would get around. We'd be labeled as a bunch of people sticking our noses into their lives.

"When anyone asks Trevor about someone's background and history, he invariably says, 'I don't know.' He doesn't know because he talks about everyday things: his motorbike, homework, and having a day off from school. Have you ever noticed how some of them have favorite phrases? Well, I noticed recently that Trevor uses them, too. There's some kind of bond in that. Remember Hammer's favorite remark? 'Don't worry about it.' " Christine and I spoke in unison, and laughed.

Later that week I learned that it's not just Trevor— all children can open doors in dealing with street people. One Friday, when Trevor's close friend Regan came along, the two of them gave a tall, thin man with a gray goatee a pillow and a piece of foam for a mattress. Delighted, the man's arms, feet, and every other joint began to move in an appreciative dance for the two boys.

When he noticed me, he slowed to a stop. I inhibited his spontaneous spirit. If it had just been the two boys, the man would have no doubt continued his celebration of having a soft place to lay his head that night.

On subsequent evenings we brought two vanloads of students from the Pennsylvania School for the Deaf along. A few weeks before, they had invited Trevor to their school and surprised him with a "Trevor Ferrell Day." Banners flew as Trevor was honored at the school assembly.

At first the street people stopped short at the sight of these youngsters signing to each other; then they accepted dishes handed out by the deaf students, watched them continue to talk with their hands, and, finally, they responded to the efforts these deaf children were making to communicate with them. Our street friends would smile encouragingly, make encouraging gestures, then start playfully to use sign language.

The twenty elementary school kids fascinated the street people with their sign language. The street people, in turn, imitated the hand motions with crazy gestures and exaggerated lip movements. At stop after stop the deaf children laughed at the gibberish the street people were communicating and, in turn, the street people laughed at themselves for acting so silly.

Another time, another visiting group—composed of mentally handicapped men and women, some in their thirties and forties—produced a series of one-on-one dramas. A proud determination shone forth as each of them cautiously, but solemnly, transported a blanket, a pair of gloves, or a pillow from the van.

The street people seemed to intuitively grasp the need of these handicapped visitors to give. Hesitant, timid, uncertain about what would happen, not a one was rejected. Each time a gift was offered and accepted, a marvelous, unrestrained expression spread over both faces—that of the giver and receiver. It was hard to watch these wrenching exchanges with a dry eye. As we drove away from each stop, the benevolent mentally handicapped volunteers waved and called out their farewells—some voices were clear, others unintelligible; but all were understood. We left behind a little food, a few warm things, and much joyful laughter. Rare, accepting love changed hands that night.

To watch the young, the handicapped, and those deprived of a home learn hospitality and enjoy each other on a street devoid of any comfort or amenity reinforced the fact that it doesn't take any special talent or ability to live. All are capable when two people are willing to peek over their private walls of isolation in order to really see the other without any protective defense.

Never was this truth so poignantly at work than in our family's relationship with Steve. A letter in the post office box began as a typical letter of support, "to commend you on the service you are providing to the poor and desperate people on the streets." By the time the letter concluded, Steve had introduced himself to us as a convict with a newfound Christian faith. "I know what it is to suffer and do without, to be looked down on and treated like you are less than human." Trevor responded, and that single page launched a constant correspondence through letters, phone calls, and cassettes. Trevor and an occasional other member of the family shared the progress and quirky, memorable episodes of the Campaign. The man behind bars prayed constantly for us and told of his ups and downs and the bitter disappointment of being refused parole.

During summer vacation from school, we decided to make the sixteen-hour drive—each way—to visit and meet Steve. Piled into the station wagon, the six of us drove all night. Once inside of the cement walls, little Trevor, unsure of what to say, stood before a big, bearded convict who also didn't know what to say.

We all made whatever small talk we could. We talked about Trevor's Campaign, and about the problems Trevor was having in school. Later, in a letter, Steve told us what our simple visit meant to him:

> I am still in a state of shock. Please forgive my ineptitude in my greetings. My mind went blank when I saw you. I had gone over our first meeting many times in my mind. About what I wanted to say and do. Then when I saw you I didn't do any of it. I doubt I can even express my feelings to you. Some of these feelings, like love, are really new to me. So I don't know how to act or what to say. Instead, I didn't do anything . . . I'm sorry, I'm not too good at showing how I feel. I'm still learning, so be patient with me. My past has had a lot of confusion, especially in dealing with emotion. It's just like crying. It's a great response to emotions, either happiness or sadness. Yet I have *never* really cried. Even when I was little. I just knew I always had to be tough.

Soon after our meeting, we received another tape. Newly assigned to a daily work detail on prison grounds, Steve was helping to build a new retaining wall that undergirded a bridge leading from the guard stations to the cell blocks. The stone pilings cemented together provided the base for the planking and beams upon which the asphalt had been poured. Steve told us how he and his inmate partner made the heavy, grueling work tolerable. "I told my buddy about you and what you are doing. We decided that each stone we haul and use represents one of the street people you feed each night. We place the stones, one beside the other, then pour the cement, which represents the constant, steady love you show them. We're rebuilding a bridge—just like Trevor is—a bridge between the haves and the have-nots."

When the bridge was completed, the builders held a dedication ceremony. Steve dropped and positioned a metal-etched plaque into the cement near the prison side. He stood back and a loud cheer broke out. "Trevor's Wall" was finished.

Steve and his friend had put together with their sweat and ingenuity a symbolic, tangible monument of what it takes to love. Visualizing the bridge in my head reminded me of what I had already seen at work in the Campaign. It doesn't take any special talent to love street people, or any other kind of person who may be different from you or me. All it takes is a willingness to do what is needed to span the distance.

9

One Step Forward,
Three Steps Back

Unobserved, I stood in the doorway of the living room at Trevor's Place. Nearly a year had passed since Father Rossi and I first turned the lock in the door and inspected the hotel. Now all of the toilets flushed—most of the time—and a majority of the faucets poured forth clear water. The kitchen efficiently provided the residents with two prepared meals a day, and they had access to its offerings until 8 P.M. every evening if they wanted anything else.

The hotel was now a home. Or was it?

What should have been a feeling of exaltation about how far we had come turned to deep discouragement. For the first time since the overwhelming day when I first saw the tasks of renovation ahead, I began to doubt the effectiveness or wisdom about this home for the homeless. I said to myself, "Frank, you've been fooling yourself. These people can't learn to live together. Look—they're turning on each other."

I was watching the regular Thursday morning meeting of the residents . . . Bob, Skinny John, Sam, June, Louis, Anne, Chico, Tom, and Harold, the house manager; all of the permanent residents were present and accounted for. Three volunteers and Janet interspersed themselves among the residents. Nancy, a social worker committed to helping us develop a group spirit, sat on a wooden chair from the kitchen at the far side of the room.

Big Bob began as he always did, by not mentioning

names. "Someone—I'm not going to say *who*—someone has been taking my food from the refrigerator. This someone who is doing this is here in this room. Now, I'm not mentioning names. But this person knows who I mean."

Then Chico added, "Yeah, this's gotta stop. This here person's been doing this before. I'm telling this person he had better stop."

Chico's agreement encouraged Bob to look in the direction of Sam, a cowering, defensive form slouched low in the overstuffed chair. Sam got up and stood in front of him. "This here person had better stop. I'm tired of warning this here person."

The room rumbled with remarks . . . "Yeah, this kind of thing can't go on" . . . "We gotta do something about this" . . . "I'm gonna watch out to see this kinda thing" . . . "Hey, it could happen to any of us here. We could be losing food" . . . "Bad stuff."

Big Bob dropped his anonymous accusation. "What about it, Sam?"

"You mean you're accusing me?"

"Yeah, he is," Chico chimed in.

Everyone was looking at Sam. They had found someone more powerless than they, someone they could strike out at. The victims had found a victim.

Nancy, who had experience in working with battered wives and troubled teenagers, stood up and planted herself in the center of the circle to neutralize the situation. "Look," she said, "we're not here to argue and to accuse each other. This has got to stop. We're here to talk about how to live together and work together. Stop, stop, stop! Let's get away from accusing each other. Let's see what we can do to help each other."

There was mostly muttering mixed with some grumbling as Nancy made everyone sit down. She steered the meeting around to the housecleaning schedule for Saturday morning. "Now we have to assign tasks. Everyone must chip in.

We will rotate the assignments so that no one person has to do the same thing every week."

She quieted the meeting, but it left me discouraged. I went outside and sat on the steps, out of hearing distance. After the meeting, I took Nancy aside and told her how I felt. She brought me down to earth. "Look, Frank, the thing you must realize is that these people are filled with anger. They feel that they are incompetent, that they can't take care of themselves. So they have the unconscious urge to dump on someone else. Given a little sense of power they feel better about themselves.

"What we have to do in these meetings is to keep the discussions in the present, to keep them task-oriented, and to establish ground rules. Only one person at a time must talk, and they all must learn to listen. We must slow each person down and reassure the group that everyone will have his or her turn to talk. Eventually, they will begin to talk and to really have a discussion."

Then Nancy looked me squarely in the eye and reminded me, "Out there in the streets, where they have no place to call their own, they are overwhelmed with a sense of powerlessness. They have no control over their own lives. They must depend on others—for handouts, for food, for shelter. Their lives are not their own. This is what we want to do for them, give them a sense of control over their environment."

She predicted, "When the group gets to feel that it truly can manage this living environment, all of the members will begin to work together. The next you'll know, Frank Ferrell, is that you have a kind of camaraderie here at Trevor's Place."

I wanted to believe Nancy, but from the first of the weekly meetings (which had started nearly three months earlier), the air was filled with what Nancy labelled "put-down stuff." Bob, one of the first residents, had acted as house manager and self-acclaimed "boss" for months until Harold, our full-time manager, came to live in Trevor's Place. So

Bob had a proprietary attitude. He bullied everyone at times, though he didn't see it that way. When confronted, he would say with a shrug, "I just want to make sure things go right. You know that, Frank."

That morning, Bob stalked across the circle from his chair and towered over Skinny John, the youngest resident in the house, who was sitting on the couch next to Janet. "That's not the way it is. Your room is horrible. You're not acting responsible. You're not taking care of your own things." He pointed his finger at Skinny John, who looked like a cornered dog about to be kicked. His lips quivered. His eyes blinked behind his thick glasses. Out of habit he looked around for a way to escape. Janet slipped a protective arm around the slim, shaking shoulders. "Don't listen to him. It's OK." She finally snapped, "Bob, that's enough," and he backed off, leaving the tender young man blushing and on the verge of tears.

So it went for five more weekly meetings until the Thursday morning when they skipped the general complaints, opting instead to begin with a discussion of Saturday house-cleaning. By then Harold was on board as house manager. A husky black man in his early thirties, Harold had come to us from the city's drop-in shelter, where he had become a more-or-less permanent resident and volunteer helper. He was a strong, firm presence and had become an anchor for life in Trevor's Place.

Harold looks like a defensive linesman for the Philadelphia Eagles. Six feet of husky muscle, he stands firm in whatever space he occupies. Harold returned to his hometown, Philadelphia, when his job in New York City folded after three-and-a-half months. He had enough money saved to move into an efficiency apartment and start looking for work. When nothing opened up he was forced to sell all he owned, and he soon found himself downtown looking for any place that would take him in. His genial nature and reliability soon led to odd jobs and other duties at the drop-in shelter. He was referred to us as the potential house manager we desperately needed.

Harold and Nancy made headway in inspiring an orderly atmosphere at the meetings, but Nancy sensed something new at this particular meeting.

"They were discussing and systematically assigning chores for Saturday housecleaning. They didn't need any guidance. They were talking constructively and fairly. I stopped them right in the midst of their discussion because I was really moved. On the verge of happy tears, I pointed out to them, 'Look at you all. Do you notice how different these meetings are from the first few times? Stop for a moment and reflect on what's happened.' "

Right away, Skinny John scooted to the edge of the sofa and spoke up, his high-pitched voice rising a note or two even higher. "We're talking to each other."

His remark stopped everyone short. An extended silence loudly spoke their agreement.

"You're right," Nancy excitedly affirmed. "The first couple of times you were like a bunch of six-year-olds. Now you're behaving like responsible adults. You're really talking to each other—and, more importantly, you're listening to each other."

As the meeting continued, the change in Big Bob's behavior was noticeable. Instead of his belligerent "I'm not mentioning any names, but . . . ," he now sat still and calmly pointed out, "Look, we got a problem here. Let's see what we can do about it."

When the group broke up, Nancy took Bob aside and asked him how he thought he was different. He paused for a brief second, then said matter-of-factly, "Well, I learned that it didn't do any good when I yelled and screamed."

Later, Nancy and I walked around the corner for a cup of coffee and talked about the needs of our residential family. As the waitress poured the steaming liquid in our mugs, Nancy succinctly verbalized what I had seen not only that day, but night after night on the streets. "Their need level is so enormous, so intense. These are people who have been pushed down and pushed down. Many of them did not feel valued in early childhood. Out of a deep insecurity, they can be very egocentric. It's me-me-me. To be sensitive to another individual is very, very tough for them. They are so very hungry for attention and acceptance themselves."

Then a question came into her eyes. "Have I ever really told you why Trevor's Place means so much to me personally? What I try to bring to any depressed group in conflict that I work with is a sense of community. I guess it comes naturally to me. I come from Amish parents and an Amish community. For me, you don't live any other way than in relationship to other people. I carry this view of life with me. I don't live in an individualistic context where it's me and me only; it's the working and struggling together that brings meaning. I think that's why I've chosen to be so involved with residential populations in my work. It's the closest I can come to professionally replicating the good in the Amish community.

"I feel strongly that no matter how hungry or how me-oriented you are, there can be a sensitization and a feeling of satisfaction from giving and exchanging with others. A group can experience the rush of really sharing, no matter how emotionally scarred and needy its individual members are. It can happen. I have tremendous faith in that fact. I've seen it happen.

"Remember, too, how tough it is to urge diehard and wary street people just to come in off the streets, and from that stage to convince some of them to take a bath. After society has cast them aside for so many years, they don't give a darn about themselves, they have lost self-esteem and the basis for trusting others. They have developed a habit of living from day to day, always uncertain, always insecure, always threatened. They find it so hard to settle down and concentrate on planning how to improve their lives. Without experiencing what they have experienced, it's hard for us to fully understand what's going on inside them. They have learned to live by mistrust and suspicion. We can't expect them to learn trust overnight."

We continued to talk. We agreed that by giving every resident we bring into the house a room to themselves and a key, we give them a place of security. Yet each one is a story with chapters of pain, defeat, rejection, struggle, suffering, shock, and—most of all—the will to survive any way they must. Some won't share their story, hiding behind a gruff manner. Others, like Chico, wait until they can trust you before they slowly reveal themselves. Many disclose the horrible and tragic details about themselves in a disjointed or even flippant way. The gaps they leave, or laugh over, reveal their inability to cope with something along the way. It all depends. June is a woman we know literally nothing about, and she's unable to tell us. Louis just laughs and says he was "hatched out in a cotton field in Norfolk." His welfare case worker claims he was born and raised in Michigan, but we'll probably never know what's really true.

As Nancy and I sat sipping our second cup of coffee, trying to piece together what we knew so that we could better understand the residents' reactions to one another, Harold joined us. A third cup was added to the table. "Sorry it took me so long to join you, I was smoothing things out between Tom and Anne," he apologized. "Why, what happened?" I asked. '

"Well, the 'special treatment' thing again. Bob doesn't think it's fair that Anne gets to use the kitchen after hours just because she's in school. He finally began to understand that if the rules are absolutely the same for everybody, regardless of a person's work or school schedule, Anne wouldn't be able to eat at all. And then as I was walking out the door . . ."

"Hold on, back up," Nancy interrupted. "Anne sure handled the criticism well this morning. She looks and acts almost like a part of the staff. What's her story?"

Harold looked at me, and I nodded. "Okay, I'll tell you what I know, Harold, you fill in where I forget."

"Let's see. I think homelessness became a shocking reality to Anne late one snowy night right after Christmas. She was new to the city, living with friends from her past—she had moved here from the Washington, D.C., area to enroll in a special medical technician program. She was out of work for six months after government cutbacks eliminated her job in some sort of social service agency, and she used up all of the unemployment benefits she was entitled to. Some sort of family violence made it impossible for her to go back and live with her natural family for long. Besides, even though she doesn't look it, she's almost thirty. So she chose Philadelphia as a place to train for a new career and make a fresh start."

"Yeah," Harold broke in. "I'll never forget the pain and determination that flashed in her eyes that morning she arrived from Temporary Resident Placement Services."

"What happened to the couple she was living with?" Nancy asked.

Her friends—hard-working, blue-collar people—failed to share Anne's conviction about needing an education. Neither of them had gone past high school, and they chided Anne repeatedly for not finding a forty-hour-a-week job, even if she had to accept minimum wage. As a single woman, with no resources to fall back on, she knew she could never live on her own with that kind of pay. But, still, they couldn't understand why a grown woman clung to the desire for a college education and a tuition grant. Her part-time job as a research assistant paid her incidental expenses. . ."

Just then, I heard Janet's voice calling my name from a few feet away. She motioned for me to scoot over, and I noticed Anne was behind her.

A little startled at being caught in the middle of her life story, I explained to Anne that I was telling Nancy how she came to Trevor's Place, since they had never really met before. "Since you're the expert on the subject, will you finish up? Explain to us why college is so important and what you felt that first night when you found yourself on the streets with no place to go."

Anne began, "After losing my job, using up my unemployment benefits and not being able to support myself, I don't ever want to be in that situation again. I want to have a skill so I can always support myself.

"The first night I was homeless I was in shock that it was happening to me. I had always lived in a middle-class home and thought of myself as removed from having to go through this sort of thing. I had even done volunteer work with the homeless one summer. After the shock of being unwanted anywhere wore off, the biggest thing was fear. I had no street smarts and I had no idea what to do in the middle of the night to be safe. I had to quickly convince myself out of the denial that this was really happening; it was a matter of survival.

"I made it through the first night on the subway and elevated train that runs all night. I was too afraid to sleep. Huddled up with my knees against my chest, I rode from one end of the line to the other, getting off, waiting on the platform, and then taking another train. I was mainly numb. I couldn't believe that this was me on the streets. I sat on the train in a daze, but at the same time watched to make sure no one grabbed my book bag or my purse. I had five or six dollars to my name.

"Since I often went early to school to study, I knew that the buildings opened at 7 A.M. So I went there and tried to get washed up. In between going to classes, I spent half of my money frantically calling all kinds of social agencies. Everyone kept telling me either they had no space or I didn't meet the criteria for their shelter. For the first time in my life it would have helped me to be either pregnant or a battered wife. I kept saying to myself, 'You've got to fight off panic. You've got to think as clearly as you can if you're going to pull through.' Finally, the Temporary Resident Shelter Services arranged for me to go to a mission shelter that's a few blocks from Trevor's Place.

"That was almost as bad as spending the night on the train. I was still too afraid to sleep and I spent most of the night crying. First of all, the place was not heated and it was the middle of January. The women and children slept in one room with rows of cots that were so close together that you had to climb over them to get to the bathroom. There was no privacy, no facilities to shower or even to wash up. They just piled us in there and ignored us, and made us leave at 6 A.M.

"I went back to the Placement Center, hungry and without sleep for two nights, clinging to my faith in God. I prayed and I prayed sitting in the waiting room. Then, I looked around and saw all the other people that needed places to stay and I started to cry again. I thought to myself, 'They can't place all of us. What's going to happen to me?' I knew I couldn't phone my family for help. They wouldn't care. I had no one to call. I had no place to turn. I felt that I was at the end of the line. But I still didn't want to give up. So instead, I went numb, refusing to think anymore.

"Then out of nowhere, a case worker with a clipboard called my name. She had a place for me to go, but warned me that it was a neighborhood like none I'd ever known before. She gave me careful instructions and told me what street corners to avoid. That's how I got to Trevor's Place. It's saved me."

Anne, usually dauntless, looked down for a moment, then turned toward Harold. "Do you think we can change the subject now? I try not to think about those days if I don't have to." He nodded.

Anne grinned and confessed, "Yesterday I asked my lab

partner to come home to study with me, but I forgot to prepare him. When he saw the sign outside telling him that this
was 'a home for the homeless,' he balked a little. I'm not
sure if he thought I was playing a joke on him or what.
When we walked inside and saw June drawing numbers
and Louis pacing back and forth mumbling to himself, he
really got nervous. Needless to say, he didn't stay very
long."

"Good thing your friend didn't visit when Don lived
here," Janet mused, then fell silent. Poor Don. We sat and
remembered the great street jester with the quick sense of
humor who turned malicious and sour after he moved into
the house. After he decided to leave, we found his room in
disastrous condition. Mutilated socks, gloves, and bedding
covered everything. The clothing he destroyed had been
donated and was stored on the first floor underneath the
stairs for distribution when it got cold. Janet and I weren't so
much angry as we were just plain sad when we saw the
waste. Who knows what inner torment prompted him?

Anne, who didn't know Don, noticed our sudden change
in mood. Perceptively she asked, "What do you do with the
disappointments when somebody does something like that
and doesn't make any progress?"

Harold took the initiative to answer. "The disappointments are frequent." Searching the rest of our faces, he
winced a little. "Remember Cassie and her baby?" Cassie
was a mentally retarded woman, the first person we had
ever taken in who had a child. She wasn't caring for the
tiny, malnourished baby, and we were relieved that they
were with us. But before we found a way to help, she moved
out during the night. After she left, Harold told us what
happened, then added plaintively, "What's going to happen
to that child?" I had never seen Harold look so helpless. It
was obvious now that the memory still got to him.

Seeing that depression was about to overtake everybody, I
decided we'd better stop the nostalgic look back at all of

those who didn't stay. "Cheer up, everybody. Look at all of your melancholy faces. Don't forget that we all knew there'd be a price to pay to help even a few regain the dignity they have lost. And that is something they will never be able to do if we don't trust them and give them responsibility—even if they don't always come through as we wish they would. We decided long ago that questionnaires and endless regulations weren't the way to go. We wanted our main message to be one of acceptance, helping them learn to make choices by giving them a place to be a part of a family, a community. So, not so much through our words but through our trust and prayers we must show each person they are valued just as they are, right now. Period. Those who leave we'll have to entrust to God."

"Hey, Frank," Nancy teased, "who was it that felt so defeated during the group meeting this morning?"

"Yes, Nancy, as usual, my little sermon is more for me than for anybody else. I have to keep reminding myself that it's one step forward and three steps back that count as progress around here. But no matter how slowly, we're getting there."

While Nancy, Janet, Harold, and I nodded together, Anne said softly, "And don't you ever forget it."

10
Sympathy Is Not Enough

"Trevor, lock your door." The door slammed and Trevor lingered for a second to try the handle. The door didn't budge. I walked along the side of the van and joined him at the back. Straight ahead swung what was left of a shattered glass sign that hung from a rusty iron rod over the entrance to a bar. The blustery wind calmed for a minute, leaving only the bitter cold.

Coming from inside the bar at the corner of Kater and 15th, the roar of the Saturday crowd told us the customers were well into the night of drinking. No one moved in the parking lot or on the adjoining street.

As the bar door opened, the dark figures of two men walked directly toward us. When they were within twenty feet or so, I noticed that one wore aviator glasses. Both wore leather jackets. There was no doubt, a confrontation was imminent.

Trevor looked up at me with a question in his eyes. I pressed my hand down on his shoulder as a cue to wait. He stopped next to me.

The one in the dark glasses made the first move. When we could begin to make out his features clearly, he abruptly thrust his hand toward Trevor. Instinctively, Trevor responded and grabbed the man's hand.

The unknown man nodded. "You're doing a great job." "Yeah," echoed his companion, who moved up and also shook Trevor's hand. "Keep it up." The pair turned around without another word and reentered the bar.

I smiled with relief at my son and exhaled audibly. "What

a difference a year makes!" I thought to myself. Just a few months ago I would have never dared to drive myself, let alone bring Trevor, into this part of town. Now, after a year and a half, all of Philadelphia is relatively safe for us. Donations and warm recognition have followed us even to forbidding corners and high crime areas.

Tonight was a rare night, reminiscent of the early days. Only Trevor and I traveled in the van. There was no carload of volunteers following us. Instead of our battered old Volkswagen van, we drove one of two brand new donated vans. One of the benefactors had told me over the phone, "Who I am is unimportant, Frank. I'll meet you in heaven." On the back of this particular van, lettering spelled out our purpose: "Trevor's Campaign: We stop to feed the homeless." And feed the homeless we had that night.

We followed our regular route. Trevor, on a whim, decided to count the number of meals we served. He kept losing count—greeting his friends and serving plate after plate kept him too engrossed to concentrate on the numbers. So, as usual, we didn't know how many scoops of chili and beans, or peanut butter and jelly sandwich halves, or hamburgers and cups of coffee we served.

On this particular night, as we do a few times a month, we made a final stop at My Brother's Place, a shelter run by Father Domenic, to deliver boxes of canned food for the nightly dinner he and his workers serve to people who walk in off the street. That's what brought us to the parking lot of the South Valley Bar.

We walked past the bar and entered the double wood doors of the building to the right. The receptionist recognized us and hollered out two workers' names before we could even say hello. Two men appeared, ready to carry in the boxes we'd left in the van. Soon the goods were delivered and I backed the van onto 15th, made a left-hand turn, and headed toward the expressway.

We had a twenty-minute drive ahead of us. As soon as we

walked into the house for a quick change of clothes, we were scheduled to head back downtown to the radio/TV complex for an interview. It would be aired live on a local network radio affiliate and videotaped for showing on cable TV at a later date. On an impulse, I said to Trevor, "OK, what questions do you think the interviewer is going to ask? Why don't you play interviewer and ask me questions?"

He straightened up in his seat and opened the glove box and pulled out a flashlight to use as a prop microphone. After a moment or two, he turned to me.

"What do you think about tonight's trip? Do you think it was worth it?" Then he positioned the flashlight under my chin.

"It's always worth it," I replied, "even if you only serve one or two people."

"What've you learned from all this?" Trevor continued.

"Good question, Trevor; let's see. For one thing, don't let what you can't do keep you from doing what you can do. But there's something else. When you see how much the street people can do without, you have a different view of what you have. Nothing is as important as you make it out to be. At the same time—this may sound strange to you— you also appreciate much more what you have. With the two of us together right now, I realize in a new way now how important times like these are."

Trevor grinned a little and put the flashlight away before he asked the next question. "What's the most important thing that's happened to you personally throughout the whole Campaign?"

"The Campaign has taught me what is really important in my life. I'm a better person than I was a year ago. But I still have a long way to go."

"What was the saddest thing that's happened?"

"The saddest thing is that I've realized there are people that nobody cares about. They've already been discarded as though they don't exist. I don't think I told you about it, but there was a city official in Florida who wanted to spray trash cans with poison. He said he wanted to do this to get rid of what he called the 'vermin' searching for food. And out in Arizona, a city passed a law saying that garbage was city property! That meant anyone trying to find food in garbage could be arrested and even sent to jail. I don't know. What do you say to people who think that way? I wish they could meet street people the way we have."

"We can pray for them, can't we?"

"Good point, Trevor, but we need to pray for ourselves, too. And not only do we need to pray, but also to turn all the injustice we see over to God. But at the same time, we can't surrender our responsibility to do something . . . to do all that we can. Do you see what I mean?"

Trevor was listening, but, as usual, he was not saying much.

As we drove along the Schuylkill Expressway, I noticed that we were almost at our exit. So I decided to turn the tables on Trevor. "My turn to ask questions," I said. "What have you learned from helping the street people?" He answered, as he always does, simply and directly:

"It's taught me that people aren't always what they seem to be. They might look mean to you, but when you go over to them, they're good, they're nice."

"What about the Campaign?"

"I'm going to keep doing this as long as I can. It's real easy to do. Anybody can do it."

We were almost to our driveway. Turning onto our street made Trevor forget the interview and tell me about the loose chain on his motorbike. He hopped out as soon as the motor was turned off and rushed to his room. Janet joined me in our bedroom. I related the mini-interview we'd just had in the van.

Watching Trevor over the months and seeing him deal with the publicity and all the attention, Janet and I remarked again on how he's remained basically the same unspoiled kid who insisted on going downtown to see for himself and give away what he could to help.

Janet sat on the bed and said, "It's amazing how he can take things in stride. Remember when the White House phoned to make a donation? It was a call from the president—or his aide anyway. All Trevor did was say, 'Oh boy, thanks a lot!' And went to his room to watch TV. He never said anything to anyone else in the family."

"You're right," I nodded. "The great thing about Trevor is that he's comfortable being who he is. I hope that we've had a hand in making him this way because we've accepted him as he is. But there's also something special here. Maybe it boils down to the fact that Trevor is so normal. He's not looking to be a superstar. Being Trevor is enough for him."

Janet admitted, "I'm so glad that Trevor hasn't left his childhood world behind. He's still absorbed in video games, TV sitcoms, and his motorbike. And all of this attention hasn't taken away his struggle with school."

We continued on the subject for a few minutes. Because of his problems with reading and schoolwork of most kinds, he's been caught between contradictory messages. In school he gets the feeling that he's not up to par with the other kids because of his lackluster grades; outside school with the Campaign, he hears that he's wonderful and very special.

"What strikes me," Janet added, "is his sense that neither view is the right one. He doesn't act as though he should get special treatment. Neither does the school's opinion make him feel second class."

By this time I was nearly dressed. As I was tying my tie in the mirror, Janet came up behind me and put her arms around me. "Do well tonight, Frank. I'll say a prayer or two for you both."

Trevor's voice broke into the warm moment. "C'mon, dad, it's time to go!"

The interviewer that night seemed to know what was in my mind. I told her how Janet and I have felt caught—

bouncing back and forth—between Trevor's education and work with the street people. Both are important for him.

"How do you help him balance the two diverse parts of his life?" she asked. The lights blinded me, and Trevor sat stiffly in the blue upholstered chair beside me. "During the school year we've limited Trevor to downtown involvement only on weekends. He knows doing his homework and working hard are essential to continue to do what he likes best."

"Who in your family has changed the most in the last year?" was her next question. "Not Trevor. Trevor has changed the least of any of us. Helping the street people doesn't seem to be a dramatic act to him. He sees it as lending a helping hand, and he certainly feels good about it. Then he goes about playing, just like any other youngster his age."

But it hadn't been nearly that simple with the rest of the family. This was confirmed when I returned home around 10 P.M. that night. The interviewer's question prompted me to take stock and discuss face-to-face what's been going on inside of Liza, Allen, Jody, and Janet, too.

I sometimes still had the feeling that my mind was entangled in fish hooks, and each of the hooks lead to a problem in Trevor's Campaign. The plumbing is messed up again at Trevor's Place. Harold says all the residents are complaining about the stench of sewage. Who's going to cook tonight? Do we have a driver for the van, or will I have to do it? Isn't there a church group scheduled to come this weekend, or are we going there to speak? What about all the people I'm supposed to call back? The TV people want to come some evening so that they can film a run. What night should that be? What are we going to do about the phone bill? It doubled this month after doubling last month.

I often wondered where my family fit amidst all of this. Last fall Allen was particularly upset by remarks to the effect that "now his father was working for Trevor." Liza was testy and sulking. Jody was whining. And Janet would remind me daily, "Don't forget you have a family to take care of."

But what about now? What I learned in talking heart-to-heart with my family—more than a year after the Campaign began—was both reassuring and hard to hear. I had to face up to what my family had been through.

Liza and I talked during what was her final term in high school. At seventeen, her mind was on what college she would attend in the fall and how she would combine her desire to be an actress with the need for a back-up career. Before we even started to talk, I took note of something wonderful. The pouting expression she had on her face only a few months before was gone.

What she said bore this out: "Three months or so ago, I was kind of resentful of the whole Campaign. I thought the Campaign itself was great, but you and Mother were never available. I couldn't stand it. I couldn't talk to you. I never could ask for anything. You were never here. I blamed you for what we were going through. I hated it.

"But now it works fine. I'm used to it. I don't feel that way at all . . . Now it feels as though our life has always been this way. It's part of my life now."

Liza explained how she had changed in a number of ways—being busy in school and at her part-time job and being away from the house most of the time herself with her own busy social life, being preoccupied with applying for college, also "starting to grow up and be more independent." Then she added:

"I think I really stopped being resentful when I started getting to know the street people, like Chico. In the first months, I didn't have much to do with the street people. I thought a few of them were real odd from what you and Mom said, but that was all. Then I met them and they're great . . . Now I see the benefits of the campaign. What it does for the street people. And I've benefitted so much. I've met such interesting people. I've broadened myself so much, meeting the street people and the different volunteers. But if you asked me about this three months ago, I would have told you, 'You're all going crazy!' "

On an impulse, I asked Liza what—many years hence—she would tell her own children about Trevor's Campaign.

"First of all, I'd explain to them how our family tends to do things on the spur of the moment. 'Cause it did just happen. It wasn't planned in the least. Then I'd probably tell them about all the different people. Then I'd tell them it was great."

When I asked Liza whether she had any advice for me, her answer touched me. "Take some time for yourself. You never take any time for yourself. When you're home, it's us kids and Mom, and when it isn't us, it's the Campaign. You don't take enough time for yourself, neither you nor Mom. You're always too busy. It's not fair to you."

Liza then added her own young woman's view of the rest of the family. "You know, Trevor and Jody are much more like me than Allen. He's the opposite of me. We get along, but we also argue a lot.

"I think Trevor's a lot like you. Both of you like to go for it. Trevor's not that way in school, but in other things he really likes to go for it. You're both very mechanical and good at fiddling with things and fixing them.

"Something else. You may not have realized how much of a hard time Trevor had at school at first. He'd come home from the school bus crying. Kids are mean. They'd tease him about being 'Mr. Superstar' or whatever. That hurt him. He's a good kid and he puts up with a lot. He's still only a twelve-year-old, even now. I feel sorry for him. He has to keep going out and giving these talks. He loves it as much as anyone working in the campaign, but he's the one who has to sacrifice most of his time. I'm glad he's doing it, but I don't think I could do it."

As Liza talked, I realized that my "little girl" had grown up almost overnight. She was already seeing her family in a new, objective perspective, including Janet. In Liza's view, "Mom really loves the Campaign and I think she's really glad it's happening. She really think it's great and enjoys working with the people. But I also think it's a strain. She not only has us four kids, but now she's also co-director of the Campaign. It's a lot of work, and you know how this family does everything—295 percent."

When I discussed the previous months with Allen, he said that at first he thought it would be another "of the family's passing fads—one of those projects we'd get involved in and soon drop." But the difference this time was "knowing that these people needed us."

Allen participates in the downtown run once a week and feels good about helping. But otherwise, he reports that there has been no noticeable effect on his school life or his relationships with his friends. Meanwhile, he continues to be an honor student and an avid fan of science fiction.

While Jody has only joined us a few times on the run— perhaps only a dozen times in the course of a year—she feels comfortable with street people. "They feel friendly to me," she says. She likes to joke with Chico and likes to serve food when she does go out in the van. Most of all, she feels close to Trevor as the one closest to her in age, and is generally oblivious of the comings and goings of the Campaign.

As for Janet, neither of us denies that we've had to make adjustments as the Campaign unfolded—or, more accurately, snowballed. One typical conversation that I recall went like this. Janet began:

"You're getting obsessed with this. You're not paying enough attention to the kids."

"I know, but if I didn't do it, it wouldn't get done. No one else is going to do it."

"You don't have to do it. The kids will be grown and then you'll say that you should have done this and that with the kids. I don't want to hear you say 'I should have.'"

"But I don't have a choice."

"But you do have a choice. You can let some of it go and have more time with the family—just like everyone else does. You know it isn't just this thing. It's your personality. This is just the way you were with the business. Now in this Campaign you are spending so much time with everyone else, with the volunteers, with all these other people. What about your own family?"

"But if I didn't take the time with all these people, they wouldn't be working with us."

Then silence and tension. The kids felt it. Janet and I felt it. I felt torn. I wanted Janet to understand that I no longer felt that I had a choice. I had to keep on helping the street people. I didn't have a plan, I had a feeling. It was more than an urge—I felt driven. And Janet was telling me to get the Campaign and myself under control.

At times, I was disheartened by what was happening in our home. Our tensions even became the subject of a front-page story in the *Philadelphia Inquirer* under the embarassing headline, "THE TOLL OF TREVOR'S CAMPAIGN—A Family Reflects on the Personal Costs of Helping the Homeless." The article particularly upset Janet and the kids. I don't blame them, since much of the article was based on what I said. I didn't feel that I had anything to hide or be ashamed of. But I can appreciate everyone else's concern about our right to privacy.

The article even reported that Janet and I had sought marriage counseling with Howard Friend, our minister and friend. As far as I'm concerned, what Howard said to the reporter was on target:

"Here's a family that lives on a quiet dead-end street, that had always lived a relatively private life, and to pretend the sudden celebrity is not gonna change that life is just naive. But at some point, there was a breakthrough, and I'm delighted. Before that, I was concerned. They all were struggling."

Well into the second year of Trevor's Campaign, I could say—not only with relief, but with a sense of celebration—that Janet and I have never been closer.

Janet can speak for herself. Even though we have talked continuously about what was happening to us and to our family, I came away with a new understanding after I asked her that night to assess what's happened to us as a family. She began by saying, "It's really worked out and things are fine now.

"The first year was really difficult, but now we've all adjusted to it. First of all, you were suddenly around all the time after all those years of going to the business six days a week. Then it was the press constantly calling and the intrusions on our privacy. All along, there was the confusion, the work to do, the demands from all directions. Things seemed to be out of control. But now we seem to have more control over the Campaign. Everything is much better."

"Now," Janet added, "I feel that this is our life. It's not alien to us. It's part of our lives."

Trevor's impulse had first brought chaos and led us close to an unforeseen avalanche of need, questioning, and tumult in our lives. It took us many months to release what once was, and embrace our new way of life. One boy had urged us into action and led us to deep changes as individuals and as a family unit. It was all normal now.

But Trevor wasn't finished. There was one more thing he needed to know.

Under Trevor's urging once again, a week later we took another step to experience even more. The kid who talked me into going downtown one cold December evening also pushed me to try on the role of a street person firsthand.

Trevor and I decided to do it together. We wanted to learn as much as we could about life on the streets. We wanted to go as far as we could in identifying with the plight of the homeless. We ended by learning more about ourselves.

For a few jarring hours, I wanted to look up from the cold

asphalt, the very location that I had looked down on in curiosity that first night. So, on a Friday night, we left our car in a parking lot on 12th Street in center city, determined to spend a night on the streets. I pocketed the keys and left my wallet under the seat. Trevor and I walked away from the car on the dark, depressing street in a chilly, damp drizzle. I was wearing my raincoat and had a couple of dollars in my pocket. A lighted sign atop a bank announced a temperature of 39 degrees. The eerie apprehension made me want to put my arm around Trevor in a protective gesture, but I held back. I felt uncomfortable with the situation—more than that, anxious. I didn't want to transmit my nervous fear to Trevor. He had a matter-of-fact attitude. He was mainly curious, judging from his demeanor.

The world looked different, so different. Just making the decision to try a night on the streets cut me off from my home. The further we were from the car, the more I felt as though I had lost my anchor.

Before we even reached the corner, I spotted a bent gold cross lying on the sidewalk. I took it as my sign that we'd be okay through the next hours. I picked up the cross and put it in my pocket.

I was struck by how different Market Street looked when we reached it. Such a familiar street, but it seemed so different from all the countless other times I've been on it. It felt as though I had never been on the street before. I didn't recognize most of the businesses advertised on the neon signs. Home never felt further away.

A few blocks and we turned into Rat Alley, where we stop every night to feed the street people. It was empty. The filth was oppressive. It felt nasty and harsh. It was desolation row.

We walked back toward Market Street. Four figures walked toward us, blocking the sidewalk. They turned out to be two couples out for the evening, talking and laughing. Suddenly, rats started racing across the sidewalk. The women screamed and scurried away. Trevor and I laughed like old hands on the street and went our way.

Next, we spent a half hour watching a thirteen-story building being demolished. It was bathed in floodlights as the giant wrecking ball pummeled the brick face of the building. Trevor wanted to see a large slab of wall come tumbling down, but he had to settle for rubble. Clouds of dust swirled all around, creating an eerie atmosphere for the two solitary spectators who were standing around because they had nothing in particular to do.

We walked toward the general area where Chico spends the night when he's on a drinking spree, and sure enough we found him—out like a light on a grate at 9th and Walnut. He was lying there with his buddy, Dave. Dave came to when we tried to rouse them, and mumbled, "Come on, Chico, wake up. Trevor's here."

Trevor was trying to nudge Chico into consciousness. The tall, huddled man didn't move at all. He kept saying, "Chico, Chico, Chico. Come on, Chico, get up." Not a sound, not even a groan.

I felt helpless standing there, watching my son plead with Chico. It was a painful sight, made all the more painful when I noticed tears running down Trevor's face. The tears mixed with the soft rain that was falling.

I have never felt closer to Trevor. At that moment, he was a child in pain—my son, my flesh and blood. At that forsaken corner on that miserable night, a special communion took place. I deeply knew what Trevor felt. We didn't have to say a word to each other. We were both lost in separate thoughts and also profoundly together in our hurt.

Reluctantly, we moved on—to 11th Street and Wendy's. We hoped that we could blend into the streets, but a policeman in a patrol car recognized Trevor and slowed down to turn the corner. He beeped his horn and called out to say hello. People lingering in doorways kept coming up to Trevor to say, "Hey, Trevor, how're you doing? Where's your van? What're ya doing?" When we told them we were going to try to stay the night, we got all sorts of invitations. We wanted to stay on our own, and the attention took some of the wind out of our sails.

Our next stop was a seamy video arcade where Trevor spent $1.25 on the games. It was an awful place, filled with smoke and the nauseating greasy smell of hot dogs and stale popcorn being cooked, heated, and reheated. When we went back onto the streets, I felt dirty, disoriented, uprooted.

We were wordlessly drawn back to Chico. But there was still no waking him.

We started to walk. There was nothing to say. We headed in the direction of our car, where we had left sleeping bags. Trevor and I said nothing to each other about our plan for the night. I didn't ask him what was running through his mind. But I was asking myself, "What are we trying to prove by sleeping on the streets for the night? Am I trying to convince myself how different it is from that first night when we came down to do something for a street person, if we could even find one? This time we're coming down to try out something that seems to have lost its point. What difference will this make? Isn't it just an empty gesture? We know how awful living here is."

Then I had the compulsion to go home. I didn't want to sleep on the wet, cold streets, even in a sleeping bag. I felt a revulsion. Maybe the admission should embarass me, but it doesn't. I prefer to identify the realization that is obvious, and absolutely overwhelming. I don't want to be without a home. To change from a person who has a place to belong to a person with nowhere to go, even for one night, is a staggering upheaval. One night, actually just a few hours, of trying out the psychological change brought such confusion and feelings of isolation. What I did or thought didn't seem to matter to anyone while I was on the streets.

Trevor and I don't have to speak on such occasions. I knew he was thinking what I was thinking.

I unlocked the doors. We got into the car without looking at each other and headed for the Expressway. We were worried about Chico, who had once again turned to the streets, leaving his bed in Trevor's Place warm and empty for yet another night of drinking. That hurt. It didn't make sense.

I also realized that the street people who offered us the hospitality of the street don't expect us to join them. They want us to acknowledge their existence, to share their humanity, to remember them. And yet to stop there leaves the pain untouched; we also have to reach out to them.

I lay in bed that night, a man more dedicated than ever to this complicated ministry that demonstrates not only that Trevor and the Ferrell family care, but that all of us who have seen and looked into the eyes of the homeless care. We want to bring them hope—not only in Philadelphia, but wherever a human being has to sleep on the streets because there is no room at any inn or in anyone's heart for them.

Looking back and looking ahead, Janet and I know deep in our hearts—as does Trevor—that feeling sympathy for the homeless is not enough. *We must do something.* It only took one cold December night to convince us of that. That is what Trevor's Campaign and Trevor's Place are all about. Anyone with an extra pillow, a used blanket, and some love can do what we do. It takes very little to bring hope.

Afterword:
The Plight of the Homeless in America

by Rebecca J. Laird*

What is a home? The answer varies with each person: "Home is where the heart is," "Home is where you hang your hat," "Home is the place I belong—where my family and those I love live." The common threads that run through all of these responses are images of familiarity, security, and stability.

David, a friend from church who helps us with our garden, was working at our home today. For most of his twenty-eight years David has drifted from place to place, sleeping in parks and occasionally accepting the temporary hospitality of a relative or friend. When I asked him what he thought a home was, he shrugged, "I don't know what home is. I never had one; maybe it's where you go to clean up."

A few minutes later, he rushed back to the table where I was writing, his eyes shining with certainty. "I figured it out! Home is having someplace to go back to. Once a year or every day, whether with friends or family. It's having someplace to go back to!"

David shed profound light on my understanding of

* Rebecca J. Laird, author of *Portraits of People in Places Not Like Home* (Kansas City, MO: Beacon Hill Press, 1982), has worked with urban missions in Paris, Sydney, and San Francisco. She has been involved in all aspects of this book including the writing and editing. She makes her home in Berkeley, CA, with her husband, The Reverend Michael Christensen, who is director of urban missions in San Francisco and Berkeley.

homelessness. A home is a refuge or harbor one can head toward when the storms of life threaten or rage. It is where one's basic needs for food, shelter, clothing, and companionship are met. It also remains, even in an age of broken homes, the center of social, educational, and moral influence. Consequently, not to experience the benefits of a home must hinder one's ability to relate to the world.

How does the lack of having a home affect people? The best way for me to understand this has been to think in terms of two of the most stress-producing events in normal life: losing a job and changing one's residence. Doctors often inquire first about the stresses in a troubled patient's life before proceeding with an exam or even a partial diagnosis. They know that stress factors alone can signal serious physical or mental crises.

What happens, then, when one moves a step beyond being laid off or fired to not being able to find a job at all? What happens when one moves, not from town to town, but from adequate living arrangements to a dumpster? What traumas are produced by these upheavals? Why should I be surprised if a ragged man in filthy clothes stands ranting nonsensically on a downtown corner? What behavior would I exhibit if five o'clock came and I had no bus or train to catch; if no car was parked for me to drive and no keys in my pocket gave me promise of entry home? Where would I rate on a stress test if I was forced to join ranks with the estimated 250,000 to 2 million men, women, and children who are homeless in America?

Trevor's Place is about these people who have learned to survive on the streets. When we look at them a little more closely, their similarities to ourselves may make us uncomfortable.

There are three major categories of homeless individuals: (1) People who sleep on the streets; (2) displaced families who live in temporary shelters, abandoned warehouses, vehicles, and so forth; and (3) residents of single-room-occupancy (SRO) hotels who have a roof over their heads, but no provisions for food, companionship, or any other amenity that makes a place to stay a home.

THE SURVIVAL MENTALITY

Homeless men and women hone and sharpen their instinct for survival. For all of them, stability is replaced by frightening vulnerability. With no place to go, curling up in a tight ball underneath a cardboard box is often the only option on a cold winter night. The will to survive is strong.

The survival mentality takes life one day at a time. Each day's task is simple: to not give up and die. Tomorrow is irrelevant until it arrives. The future may encompass the next week, but probably not much more.

PURCHASING SELF-RESPECT

The need for personal dignity is closely connected to the survival mentality. Without a modicum of self-respect, the soul shrivels. Like their middle-class brethren, who may unwisely spend their paychecks on the latest model car instead of putting money into a savings account, the poor and homeless seek approval from others by buying unneeded— dearly wanted—things. So instead of using the government-subsidized monies to buy groceries, a man purchases a pair of hand-crafted cowboy boots. He doesn't need them; a number of local missions could supply him with good shoes. He buys the boots for status. Each time he looks down at the shiny boots, they tell him that he *is* somebody, even though society says he is a jobless, irresponsible nobody. These boots make him feel better than the others on the streets, with their worn hand-me-down shoes. Like many of us, he spends his hard-earned money on his self-image and not on long-term interests. When you are not sure whether you will survive beyond today, it is hard to think of tomorrow. We must understand this distinction when we explore the plight of the homeless; we must look beyond the lifestyle to see the needy person within.

HOW THE GOVERNMENT RESPONDS

Unfortunately, government programs don't address the people on the streets as human beings who need to purchase self-respect as much as a sandwich and a glass of milk. Multiple millions of dollars are spent to provide assistance for the poor through Supplemental Security Income, Disability Insurance, and various state and local assistance funds. Despite the money that is allocated, the fact remains that a huge breakdown occurs because one must spend endless hours standing in lines and filling out forms to receive the promised resources.

In order to get public assistance, the needy must appear early, stand in line before the offices open, and hope to be one of the lucky few to file through and be processed before closing time. Meanwhile, they have missed both the Salvation Army's breakfast and the soup kitchen's lunch. More tragically, by the time they've crisscrossed the city on a number of buses, they are too late to stand in line for bed tickets at city shelter programs. Housing vouchers are usually depleted by six o'clock each evening.

Adding to the depersonalization of the poor, many city social workers have become monitors of the system's resources rather than advocates for the homeless. Overburdened by work themselves, they have little sympathy for the fatigue and anger of their clients. There is no easy way out of this bureaucratic maze.

New York City, for example, is a systematized nightmare. Innumerable investigative reports reveal that exorbitant sums of money—$12,000 to $14,000 per month—are spent to house families in single rooms in filthy, rundown hotels. The same family of four would receive a welfare rent subsidy barely topping $200 if they found an apartment on their own. City rents range from $300 per month for a one-room studio without utilities in a crime-ridden area to well over $1,000 for a clean, safe space. Allocating money is not enough. There needs to be a way to ensure it is being properly spent on the homeless and not drained away by ineffective programs.

The futility of depending on the system leads to a profound sense of powerlessness. If you want to get help you are at the mercy of rules and regulations. You have to wait your turn. Many of the homeless have been waiting for help all of their lives. In order to relieve feelings of helplessness and impotence, some take matters into their own hands. Anger, rage, and violence are the results.

Conversely, it is true that many people abuse the system trying to get extra for themselves. Social workers who have been conned a number of times often become immune to the sad stories. However, a New York City social worker revealed that of all the women clients she has seen in the last four years—she sees an average of sixty a day—only one was determined to defraud the government. But for every one like her, there were more than five thousand women desperate to find the means to survive.

Each person in need who sits across the desk from a social worker craves to hear a word of hope, even a dim promise that life's situation might someday get better. Still, both the social worker and the needy individual must face the reality that there are too many with problems and too few tangible resources available.

THE HOMELESS SOCIETY

It is no wonder, then, that many who confront the daunting obstacles to obtaining aid opt instead to join the society of the homeless. There is no red tape and only one eligibility requirement: no place else to go.

Life on the streets, like life anywhere, has a social structure. Most join a small band of others in like circumstances. If you drink, you drink with other alcoholics. If you do drugs, so do your friends. If you're a single mother with children, you accept temporary housing in an SRO hotel with other desperate families. The powers that be may seem to care very little, but your street family will take care of you. If you don't have a bottle of wine, a fix, or food for your children, one of your brothers or sisters in need will share.

One of the greatest paradoxes of street life and the survival mentality is the nearly universal willingness of those with meager means to share with those who have nothing. Although survival ultimately means "me first," there is still room for those in one's surrogate family. A poignant TV report in the winter of 1984 recounted a donation to World Vision's fund to aid the starving in Ethiopia. The men of skid row in Los Angeles collected more than $150 to aid those more needy than themselves.

Beyond sharing resources, the homeless find themselves mutually caring for each other's children. In SRO hotels, mothers take turns heading toward job interviews and agency lines, while another stays behind to watch the kids. Women in the society of the homeless take care of each other, since no one else is willing to.

WHO ARE THE HOMELESS?

In Chapter 4 of *Trevor's Place* we met Sonny, Carlos, and Juan. Their stories reveal the main reasons people become homeless survivors, but there are innumerable others. A 1984 report compiled by UCLA researchers in Los Angeles, a county with 38,000 homeless, garnered data from in-depth interviews with 238 homeless persons at soup lines and shelters. Forty percent had completed at least one year of college, close to the educational norm for the total county population. The median age was thirty-seven, and nearly half were military veterans. Three-fourths were male, but the number of women was steadily increasing. Two-thirds spent less than a year actually on the streets before finding a more suitable environment.

In my research and work with the homeless in San Francisco, I have found seven primary factors leading to homelessness. The numerical breakdown for each of these causes is unknown, and most individuals fall easily into more than one category.

Substance abuse is an obvious factor. More and more of the young, entrapped by adolescent addiction, filter through the streets. They are no longer welcome in the homes where their drug abuse has damaged relationships and severed ties. Consumed with the need to obtain drugs, life on the streets allows for little judgment, easy access, and the assurance of being surrounded by a group of those with like dependencies. These young join the older alcoholics, mixing booze and drugs. Substance abuse is no longer just a problem for the winos with red noses and oversized shoes. It affects all ages and cuts across socioeconomic strata.

Mental illness is a fact of life in every major metropolitan area: a bag lady mumbles to herself, a street orator rants violently, a young man sits huddled and scared in an obscure corner. The de-institutionalization of hundreds of thousands of hospitalized patients has rendered a majority of the mentally ill homeless. Months of life on the streets also causes the otherwise well-balanced to snap, compounding the problem.

Broken family ties are often a part of rootlessness. Battered wives and abused children flee from homes where a dominant figure usually controls the household. Unable to survive there, they take flight without money or support, knowing they can never return. Marital breakups leave the children at the mercy of parents in personal chaos, who are then unable to support or care for them. Unwanted by either parent, these children too hit the streets. Drifting, prostitution, and crime are common last resorts for these who are too young to find legal jobs. Their fathers and mothers, cut off from familial identity, can easily drift into the streets feeling unwanted and without means of support.

Poverty, plain and simple, also leads to homelessness. When a person lives from paycheck to paycheck, the loss of a job or afffordable apartment leaves no alternative to homelessness. When one is unskilled, with no job experience to fill a resume, job hunting becomes nearly impossible.

The elderly on fixed incomes are especially susceptible to resourceless poverty. Beyond working age, they have no hope of increasing income to cover increased expenditure demands. Urban ghettos, barrios, projects, and retirement hotels are only one tiny step away from the streets.

The resurgence of corporate business in the cities is another seldom-considered contributor to homelessness. New York City is estimated to have lost 90,000 jobs since 1980, as companies have moved to the suburbs. At the same time, 140,000 new jobs have opened up. That sounds like good news, but in fact it is devastating news for the poor. Of those new jobs, nearly all are for white-collar executives and blue-collar skilled professionals. The laboring class that was employed by the factories and industrial warehouses that moved out of the city is completely unqualified for the new employment opportunities. The laborers have no savings or means to relocate near suitable job markets.

Gentrification, a result of the need to house the newly employed corporate workers, compounds this problem. Landlords know that a renovated building will bring higher rents and appeal to the higher wage earners. Evicting current residents to cater to more affluent renters is a frequently made, pragmatic choice. Unemployment coupled with eviction equals homelessness for the urban poor.

The choice to be homeless, though we may find it difficult to understand, is often made willingly. In the 1980s, many people calling themselves punk rockers, new wavers, skinheads, and anarchists have replaced the hippies and flower-children of the 1960s. Disillusioned by the entrepreneurial lifestyle of getting ahead in America, they choose to join quickly formed communities in abandoned city buildings. Scouring city records for empty buildings that may be legally susceptible to squatter's rights provisions, they move in to inhabit the building and stake a claim until they are thrown out by police or the landlord. Those who don't wish to be a part of the fight for squatter's rights may form a community of tents in a public park or an encampment of old buses. Reminiscent of the pioneer days, these renegade groups hang onto the dream of forming a new, communal utopia.

WHAT CAN BE DONE TO HELP?

The problem of homelessness in America seems to be out of control. As a result, everyone blames everyone else. The cities point a finger at state hospitals for discharging mental patients without ensuring proper and continual care. The state blames the city for establishing housing policies in the 1970s to encourage urban renewal—the conversion of aging buildings that housed the poor into condominiums and premium office space. And everyone blames the federal government. Only the federal government has the resources to relocate hundreds of thousands of people and find a way to enable them to stay in one place long enough to learn skills, find day care, and seek jobs so that one day they may be able to shelter, feed, and support themselves.

Recently, all three levels of government have found another group to focus some of the responsibility on: The private sector—churches, synagogues, and charitable organizations have always tried to care for society's oppressed. These efforts exist mainly on charitable contributions and operate outside of the realm of federal funding.

Paradoxically, these private programs are not being recognized as the most economically feasible means of help.

Their costs for overnight housing are often five times less than that of city agencies, which have employment quotas and union wages to contend with. Most private facilities can house, clothe, and feed individuals for $6,000 per year. Mental hospitals' costs top $40,000 per patient annually. City shelters in armories or gymnasiums cost $20 to $40 per person per night—$10,000 a year. And in cities like Chicago, where 100 city-operated beds are available for the 20,000 homeless, the cost is irrelevant to the unmet, immediate needs.

If the complex problems of homelessness are ever to be alleviated, we must rid ourselves of the notion that government alone can remedy the situation. But the government can't simply acknowledge this fact and cut back monies. Instead, those funds may need to be channeled to the support and establishment of private organizations. And the public will have to quit waiting for a policy miracle to be passed by Congress.

We must finally come to a place where we cannot tolerate the idea that the brothers, sisters, children, and parents of this nation have no roofs over their heads or food in their stomachs. We must become involved. In late 1984, New York's Mayor Koch pleaded with churches and synagogues to involve themselves in the plight of the poor. He promised beds, linens, and food if space and volunteer staff could be provided by the private sector. Only thirty-nine, a tiny portion of the city's thousands of religious organizations, responded. New York, the city with both the largest homeless population in America and the most active aid programs, spent $170 million in one year on homelessness, and hardly made a dent.

Cooperation between public and private efforts is essential.

Creative ways to aid and train the homeless are endless. There are already many private organizations that help the homeless. Aid may range from immediate shelter to helping individuals locate an apartment, finance the move-in costs, and subsidize the first six-month's rent until the person is stabilized.

One group, which specializes in helping women in need, has a clothing room filled with coordinated outfits—from shoes to jackets—garnered from donated, used clothing. Each time one of the women has a job interview, she is allowed to choose her attire so that she can present her self in proud fashion. After the interview, she returns the clothing so that another may have the same fair chance.

TEN WAYS TO HELP THE HOMELESS

Individuals must also find ways to help. The Ferrell family has compiled a list of ten ways each person can become a part of the solution to homelessness.

1. PRAY for the homeless and those striving to help them.
2. RESEARCH what is being done in your own area in city/state/community efforts. Look into volunteer organizations, such as the Salvation Army and Red Cross, and into Protestant, Catholic, and Jewish organizations that may have soup kitchens or shelters and hospices for the homeless.
3. HELP WITH FOOD by collecting and/or cooking for shelters and hospices. Ask church and school groups to get involved.
4. COLLECT CLOTHING, particularly warm coats, woolen hats and scarves, socks, shoes, boots, sweaters, and gloves. Take these things to the street people yourselves (always go in groups, never alone) or donate them to organizations serving the homeless.
5. BUY OR COLLECT household items, particularly blankets, sleeping bags, and pillows. Also sheets, toothpaste, toothbrushes, soap, washcloths, and shampoo (a luxury). Distribute them directly or through groups.

6. KNOW AND GIVE WITNESS. Become familiar with the reasons why people end up on the streets and foster respect for them, despite their situation. Stress *life itself* as the highest value, rather than an individual's status in life. Defend the rejected members of our society from the "throwaway mentality." Help to make street people visible as God's children just as much as anyone else. Put human beings—all human beings—above things. Sensitize yourself to others in need. Realize how easy it is to respond the way the editors of a Florida newspaper did in the midst of a winter freeze that imposed heavy losses on the orange crop. That was front-page news. Buried inside the newspaper at the bottom of a page amidst supermarket ads was an item about eight people freezing to death during the same cold spell!

7. SPEAK OUT on behalf of the homeless in organizations you belong to, write your local newspapers about the plight of the homeless, let editors know that their readers care and want editors to notice the homeless at their downtown doorsteps.

8. CALL for government action on behalf of the homeless. Don't expect city, state, and federal governments to solve the problem overnight; but call for legislation, research, and official actions that respond to the problem that has become the hallmark of center city in America. As one lawyer working for the homeless has said, Americans "must address the question of whether human beings in the U.S. have a right to better shelter than a dumpster."

9. JOIN individuals and groups who are helping the homeless. If you can't join, help in whatever way you can— with donations of money, clothing, food. Whatever you can do, DO.

10. CARE. You will make an incredible discovery. You are not alone. As we have learned with what began as our

small gesture, people everywhere are waiting to respond. They want to become part of a chain of CARING that is growing stronger all the time.

Soup kitchens, temporary housing facilities, and de-tox units nationwide report a swelling number of those requesting services. Most report serving one-third more in 1984 than they did in 1980.

In multiple conversations with those who work daily with the poor in America, one consensus opinion surfaces: homelessness will be in the forefront of social problems of the 1980s and 1990s. Statistically, the problem is already daunting and immobilizing.

This brings us back to where the Ferrells began. One family opened the door of their home to a few who had no place to go. By offering trust, dignity, security, love, and most importantly, time, some people who were homeless aren't anymore. One to one help is the best way to bring hope to the homeless. Trevor began with a simple act and a willingness to learn. We can too.

CHRISTIAN HERALD ASSOCIATION AND ITS MINISTRIES

CHRISTIAN HERALD ASSOCIATION, founded in 1878, publishes The Christian Herald Magazine, one of the leading interdenominational religious monthlies in America. Through its wide circulation, it brings inspiring articles and the latest news of religious developments to many families. From the magazine's pages came the initiative for CHRISTIAN HERALD CHILDREN and THE BOWERY MISSION, two individually supported not-for-profit corporations.

CHRISTIAN HERALD CHILDREN, established in 1894, is the name for a unique and dynamic ministry to disadvantaged children, offering hope and opportunities which would not otherwise be available for reasons of poverty and neglect. The goal is to develop each child's potential and to demonstrate Christian compassion and understanding to children in need.

Mont Lawn is a permanent camp located in Bushkill, Pennsylvania. It is the focal point of a ministry which provides a healthful "vacation with a purpose" to children who without it would be confined to the streets of the city. Up to 1000 children between the age of 7 and 11 come to Mont Lawn each year.

Christian Herald Children maintains year-round contact with children by means of a *City Youth Ministry*. Central to its philosophy is the belief that only through sustained relationships and demonstrated concern can individual lives be truly enriched. Special emphasis is on individual guidance, spiritual and family counseling and tutoring. This follow-up ministry to inner-city children culminates for many in financial assistance toward higher education and career counseling.

THE BOWERY MISSION, located at 227 Bowery, New York City, has since 1879 been reaching out to the lost men on the Bowery, offering them what could be their last chance to rebuild their lives. Every man is fed, clothed and ministered to. Countless numbers have entered the 90-day residential rehabilitation program at the Bowery Mission. A concentrated ministry of counseling, medical care, nutrition therapy, Bible study and Gospel services awakens a man to spiritual renewal within himself.

These ministries are supported solely by the voluntary contributions of individuals and by legacies and bequests. Contributions are tax deductible. Checks should be made out either to CHRISTIAN HERALD CHILDREN or to THE BOWERY MISSION.

Administrative Office: 40 Overlook Drive, Chappaqua, New York 10514
Telephone: (914) 769-9000